JUST LEAD!

BREAK THROUGH THE OVERWHELM AND LEAD WITH IMPACT

DALE MONK

For Olivia. You inspire me every day. You are smart, powerful, passionate, caring and beautiful. I love you and I am so very proud of you.

From everyone who has been given much, much more will be demanded; and from the one who has been entrusted with much, much more will be asked.

– Luke 12:48

First published in 2021 by Dale Monk

A catalogue entry for this book is available from the National Library of Australia.

ISBN: 978-1-922553-58-4

Project management and text design by Publish Central
Cover design by Pipeline Design

Contents

Introduction

I've been there – done that! I know what it's like to be promoted to a leadership role only to realise, to your horror, that you might be out of your league – wondering whether you're on the brink of failure and humiliation. In my desperation as a new leader, I stumbled on some principles that not only helped me to survive the leadership challenges I faced, but to thrive and grow into an impactful leader. It was reassuring to discover that effective leadership can be as simple as embracing your own authentic style, rather than trying to make sense of all the theories, training and opinions of others that don't necessarily work for you. My aim in writing this book is to pass those lessons on to you, the reader. Some I learned through trial and error, others through timely input from gifted and experienced leaders who took the time to invest in my professional life.

In *Just Lead!*, I'll teach you how to unlock your unique potential as a leader by providing simple, easy-to-implement principles that will help you connect with your own leadership style. I'll encourage you to stop trying to emulate others – this only results in frustration, both for you and those you lead. Instead, you'll learn to flow with what your creator has already put in you – unearthing your own natural leadership bent.

Just Lead! is not one of *those* leadership books – you know the type: written by an academic with little practical experience. Instead, it is the book all leaders wish they had read before they accepted the gig, written by a leader who has learnt, through trial and error, what amplifies impact and influence.

Let the Sunday school story of David and Goliath be your inspiration. Before David engaged Goliath the giant in battle, David's king intervened. Thinking he was doing the young lad a favour, the king offered to lend David his armour and personal weapons. David, in deference to his king, tried the armour and weapons but quickly realised they wouldn't work for him. He instead wisely engaged his enemy with what he knew was more in line with his natural gifting: no armour for protection, and only a slingshot for a weapon. The rest is history. He vanquished the giant.

No doubt you have achieved a level of success to date that has provided the foundation for a successful career; but you might be thinking, 'Will I ever become the leader I aspire to be?'. I have written this book for you – to make you a better, more impactful, more influential leader. There isn't a one-size-fits-all approach to leadership. How brilliant is that? This means we can be ourselves – authentic, at our best and positively impacting others.

So, together, let's start finding your leadership style.

The impactful leader's manifesto

It's time we got real about leadership. The impactful leader's manifesto is my proverbial line in the sand. Intentionally causing a ruckus and instigating change, I've written this manifesto to represent who I am and what I stand for. Leadership is a personal journey and yet we have somehow managed to force a model for decades without success. This must change.

THE MANAGERIAL TAILSPIN

I first met Michelle at a cafe. She was 15 minutes late and flustered, having rushed from her previous meeting. She sat down, ordering a latte as she caught her breath. Michelle's CEO had suggested we work together. Following her internal promotion to the role of director, Michelle had spent the previous 12 months experiencing a rollercoaster of emotions. I asked Michelle how she was, and a stock-standard reply of 'busy' followed a slow, deep sigh. Michelle started to tell me how she missed her previous role. It was a role in which she was very comfortable – a trailblazer, pioneering a path of outstanding achievement. Her performance was the reason she landed the director role. It was her dream job. 'This is the role I am supposed to have,' she said, 'and yet, I just can't seem to win. Every day is like Groundhog Day. I start the day with the best of intentions, but no matter how early I start or how late at night I am up writing reports, I can't seem to keep my head above water. I am forever putting out fires, most of which are not mine. It's my team. I feel that

I am not delivering, and it is only a matter of time before they catch me out. I don't know where to start to get back on track. I feel so overwhelmed.' I could see that she was emotionally exhausted and yet relieved to share her feelings. Michelle was in what I have come to call a managerial tailspin, and her fears were making matters worse.

Let me explain what I mean by managerial tailspin. It's when you have reached the pinnacle of your career, but find it is not what you expected. Promotion to a leadership position was the natural next step in your well-established career; however, while it brings more money and respect, the role of leader fails to light you up as your previous job did. Reality sees you working harder than you ever did before without making much progress, doing tasks that you do not enjoy. You have spent your career refining your craft and building a reputation for excellence, only to find yourself depressed and disappointed. Being a leader is not all it's cracked up to be! You slide from star expert to floundering pessimist and cling for dear life to the elements of your old role you loved in your search for satisfaction. Falling into the trap of meddling, you never take the reins of your leadership role, leading to complaints from staff, peers, executives and stakeholders. Consumed by fear, you doubt your ability to deliver to expectations.

Here is the good news: this feeling is common. Almost every leader has experienced overwhelm. Some take action to improve their leadership skills; picking up this book is a great first step towards exactly that.

LEADERSHIP DEFINED

Google 'what is leadership?' and you'll get some 906 million results. No wonder organisations, leaders and followers alike struggle to know what leadership actually is. Among the millions of entries are famous quotes on the topic:

- 'Leadership is not a person or a position. It is a complex moral relationship between people based on trust, obligation, commitment, emotion and a shared vision of the good.' – Joanne Ciulla, American philosopher and pioneer in the field of leadership ethics

- 'Leadership is the capacity to translate vision into reality.' – The late Warren Bennis, global leadership expert, accomplished author and lecturer and strategic adviser to four US presidents

- 'If you can get people to follow you to the ends of the earth, you are a great leader.' – Indra Nooyi, former CEO and chairman of the board at PepsiCo Inc; Nooyi was instrumental in the lucrative restructuring of the soft drink manufacturer resulting in significant organisational growth during her tenure

- 'A great leader is someone who makes their employees feel safe, who draws people into a circle of trust.' – Simon Sinek, acclaimed author of five books including *Start With Why: How Great Leaders Inspire Everyone to Take Action*

- 'Leadership is about making others better as a result of your presence and making sure that impact lasts in your absence.' – Sheryl Sandberg, COO at Facebook and the acclaimed author of *Lean In: Women, Work, and the Will to Lead*; the first female elected to serve on Facebook's board of directors

- 'The only definition of a leader is someone who has followers.' – Peter Drucker, the most widely known and influential thinker on management; Drucker's work continues to be applied by managers worldwide

- 'If your actions inspire others to dream more, learn more, do more and become more, you are a leader.' – John Quincy Adams, sixth president of the United States.

As impressive as these quotes are, they merely reflect the journey of the leader – the leader's experiences, expertise and challenges. These quotes do not, however, *exactly* define what a leader does.

The *Macquarie Dictionary* defines leadership as the position, function or guidance of a leader; the ability to lead. The *Collins English Dictionary* defines leadership as the people who are in control of a group or organisation. Let me quickly grab a fork to gouge my eyes out. These definitions are incredibly uninspiring.

LEADERSHIP *IS* MANAGEMENT

When did it all become so complicated? I blame Professor Abraham Zaleznik – well, 'blame' is a strong word. His 1977 *Harvard Business Review* article 'Managers and Leaders: Are They Different?' created the divide between leadership and management. Professor of leadership at Harvard Business School and the author of many books and articles, Zaleznik is one of the few certified psychoanalysts in the United States without a medical degree. He asserted that management and leadership are two different beasts: management seeks order, control and the rapid resolution of problems; leaders, on the other hand, are like artists who tolerate chaos and a lack of structure. In his groundbreaking article, Zaleznik argued that the traditional view of management failed to recognise the leadership essentials of inspiration, vision and human passion. He, therefore, suggested organisations needed both managers and leaders to be successful.

Zaleznik is a credible voice in leadership expertise; however, his article confused the role of leader and the function of management. He merely articulated the essential attributes of influence and impact. The distinction between leadership and management was unnecessary. There is no leader who does not manage. Simply delivering a vision of the future, in itself, is not leadership. You need to communicate and engage the vision and possess the authority to make decisions about the resources that make that vision a possibility.

To deny the fusing of leadership and management is utter nonsense. Leadership cannot exist without management. Management is not the opposite of leadership. Leadership is the influence that motivates and enables others to contribute towards success, while management controls resources to support objectives.

THE LEADERSHIP DILEMMA

Most of us are not natural-born leaders. American analytics and advisory company Gallup found that 82 per cent of leaders are not very good at leading people. Gallup spent two decades surveying almost 27 million employees globally – across more than two million work units from diverse organisations and sectors. They found that, even over those 20 years, there was little change in leadership effectiveness.

Leadership training as a global industry was worth around $510 billion in 2019. That is Australian dollars, by the way! Despite this significant investment in people leaders, leadership skills are deteriorating. Barbara Kellerman, author of *Bad Leadership: What It Is, How It Happens, Why It Matters*, says, 'There is precious little evidence that the leadership industry has, in any meaningful, measurable way, benefited society.' Ouch! According to *Training Magazine*, a global training and workforce development publication, 85 per cent of businesses surveyed intended to either maintain or increase their leadership development investment into 2021 – despite the continued impacts of the coronavirus pandemic on global economic conditions. I believe we are spending the right amount of money on our leaders' development – it is just poorly invested.

In 2010, Resoomay, a now-defunct boutique recruitment agency based in New York, identified that a lousy leader could cost their organisation up to $1 million Australian dollars. (You might question a defunct firm's credibility, but their misfortune was caused, in part, by spending a lot of money on this kind of research.) Costs related to poor leadership include:

· lost remuneration
· termination costs
· new recruitment costs
· costs related to restoring employee morale and productivity
· costs of rectifying mistakes
· missed business opportunities.

Poor leaders can sometimes fly under the radar, with these costs only realised many years into their tenure. Unfortunately these costs can continue to affect an organisation for many years after their termination.

You only need to turn on the television, read the newspaper or look around the office to see yet another example of poor leadership, poor decisions and poor behaviour.

According to global executive outplacement services firm Challenger, Grey & Christmas, Inc, 2019 saw the highest level of CEO turnover since data reporting began in 2002. A significant number of these departures were the result of inadequate – sometimes toxic – leadership. The Ken Blanchard Companies, a global leadership consultancy established to enhance the positive impact of leadership, found poor leadership costs the typical organisation an amount equal to 7 per cent of their total annual sales. The consultancy's 2020 report, *7 Ways Leaders Are Costing Your Company Money*, also found that better leadership can eliminate as much as a third of an organisation's voluntary turnover. Bad leadership is causing everyone pain. It is a vicious cycle of overwhelmed leaders who feel lost and unsupported, teams that fail to reach their full potential and organisations on the perpetual and unreachable path to greatness.

Linda Hutchings, one of New Zealand's most respected adult educators in leadership development, once said that leadership is your second career. This is a truth very few leaders acknowledge. It took me five and a half years to complete my bachelor's degree. No, I am not a slow learner; I worked full-time for the majority of my studies. After graduation, I enrolled in the CPA Australia program. Three and a half years later, I was qualified to be doing the job I had done for almost five years. To be an accountant, I invested nine years and $75,000 in learning the ropes, gaining technical competency and applying my skills – and that does not include the financial outlay for continuing professional development. I was very good at what I did, and my career advancement was quick. Deep down, though, I wouldn't say I loved the numbers. I was bored to tears by accounting standards and financial statements. I was a square peg in a round hole.

I learnt early on that to be a successful leader, I needed to develop my skills. That meant I invested in my leadership capability and did not wait for the organisation I was working for to do so. According to micro-learning company Grovo, 44 per cent of first-time leaders feel unprepared for their new role, with 87 per cent wishing they had undertaken more training before becoming leaders. Alarmingly, in my research on the professional development of leaders, I discovered that some leaders are in their positions for as long as nine years before participating in a leadership development program. This is a case of too little, too late. You cannot teach a skydiver how to deploy a parachute after having jumped out of a plane. Compared to your investment in your technical skills, how much have you invested in developing your leadership skills? Do not wait for your employer to take responsibility for your leadership aspirations. Leadership is a lifelong journey, and you need to be in the driver's seat.

I feel for those in human resources. They have the short end of the stick. Some organisations appear to have a drug-like dependency on their HR departments, with CEOs turning to them to plug gaps in skill sets, leadership capability and succession planning. Over time, they have been lumped with all of the people issues and rarely have the capacity to assess the abilities and gaps of management – let alone implement a talent-management strategy. Consequently, generic leadership training is rolled out to people leaders to meet the demand for professional development.

Flashbacks to the leadership training I endured in my career still invoke eye-rolling. Emotional intelligence, managing performance, courageous conversations, time management – the list goes on. You cannot fill your face with muffins, step into a scenario using a 10-step process with trained actors, and expect reality to be so abiding. By the time you have realised you are in the middle of a difficult conversation, it is usually too late to employ your training – you have forgotten your script, and it all goes off the rails. No wonder some organisations see little to no tangible benefit from their significant investment in leadership training.

You may have worked with, or alongside, an overwhelmed leader forced to develop their people skills. By forced, I mean that leadership development has been imposed on them by HR, usually as part of a performance improvement plan. Rather than taking an organisational-wide investment in leadership capability, this reactionary approach to skill-building may be seen as a punishment. Sadly, a leader in this situation may feel shrouded in secrecy and shame. Leadership development can be less effective when delivered to a single person.

I have seen firsthand the significant returns to organisations that openly promote and encourage their people's development journeys. But I get it – developing a tailored leadership program takes time, energy and money. I empathise with organisations that see this task as a bottomless pit. However, I have also seen proven time and time again that a robust leadership development program is significantly cheaper than the cost of employee relations management, staff turnover, employee disengagement, terminations and talent attraction and retention.

It reminds me of the joke about the CEO and the CFO who are challenged by the 'damned if we do, damned if we don't' leadership dilemma of balancing investment and tangible returns. A CEO tells the CFO that the organisation needs to increase its investment in employee development. 'What happens if we spend the money to train them and they leave?' asks the CFO. 'What if we don't train them and they stay?' replies the CEO. Talented employees do not leave organisations due to newly developed skills; they leave despite this. Employees leave because of a lack of learning and development opportunities in their organisation. They seek to grow in their contribution to their organisation; if they find this is not possible, they start to look elsewhere.

I want to make it clear that I *am* having a go at the way we have done things in the past – leadership 'trainers' and HR departments alike. We need to realise the current approach is not working and that we need a new way. Let's redirect the financial investment and be more effective. I advocate for leadership mentoring tailored to the individual, focusing on leveraging strengths and optimising weaknesses.

LEADERSHIP IS A DANCE

According to *Harvard Business Review*, leadership scholars have spent the last 60 years conducting more than 1,000 studies to determine the definitive styles, characteristics and personality traits of great leaders. None of these studies have been able to produce a clear profile of the ideal leader.

There is a need to define leadership – but the vague, nebulous affirmations that people throw at us, like the list of quotes that I gave you earlier, are not helpful. Leadership is a very personal concept. But how can there be a need to define leadership, and yet the very definition is personal and reflective of our view of the world, shaped by our values, experiences and expectations? Leadership is like a dance. A dance has steps – yet the dance partner, the music and the environment are all variables you need to accommodate. A gifted dancer knows how to leverage each element. At the start, it may be clunky, but with practice and perseverance, it is elegant.

I believe leadership is embarking on the journey of possibility – harnessing others' untapped brilliance to reach beyond expectations by doing the best things at the best time and in the best way. However you define it, you must be able to articulate what leadership means to *you*. It will be the yardstick against which you will be measured, and it will guide your future development. Therefore, effective leadership is the alignment of your unique definition of leadership and the objectives of your organisation.

LEADERSHIP AWARENESS

1

First, lead yourself

Awareness is like the sun. When it shines on things they are transformed.

– Thich Nhat Hanh

When clients first start working with me, it's often the case that they've received feedback from their manager about needing to develop their emotional intelligence. 'So, when do we do that?' is often asked in haste.

Most of us have heard of emotional intelligence. Some people know what it is. Few people realise that you cannot develop it overnight.

Daniel Goleman, psychologist and author of *Emotional Intelligence: Why It Can Matter More Than IQ*, pioneered the idea that 'the ability to recognize and understand your moods, emotions, and drives, as well as their effect on others' is a hallmark of influential leaders. Goleman was not the pioneer of the psychological theory of emotional intelligence; emotional intelligence as a psychological theory was developed by psychologists Peter

Salovey and John Mayer. Goleman, however, popularised the concept of emotional intelligence and the impact it has on successful human relationships.

Emotional intelligence is the ability to understand and manage your own emotions and the emotions of those around you.

People with a high degree of emotional intelligence know what they are feeling, what their feelings mean and how their emotions can affect others. According to Goleman, emotional intelligence comprises five essential elements – self-awareness, self-regulation, motivation, empathy and social skills. A 2010 study by the Cornell School of Industrial and Labor Relations found self-awareness to be the strongest predictor of overall success. Developing self-awareness as a leader is the first step in developing emotional intelligence and the most challenging leadership skill. It is a lifelong process of continual reflection. It is never too late to develop your emotional intelligence, and there are 40 thousand reasons why! Research by TalentSmartEQ, a provider of emotional intelligence training and development, found leaders with high levels of self-awareness earn, on average, $40,000 more than leaders who lack personal insight, understanding and control.

Self-awareness is the capacity to honestly evaluate your values and beliefs, actions and impact on others. It is about understanding what makes you, you. Who you are as an individual shapes your leadership style. The secret to gaining self-awareness is exploring your leadership blind spots. By blind spot, I mean any area of your leadership where you continually fail to realistically and without bias see yourself or your situation. This unawareness can seriously damage your credibility.

EMULATION CAN BE DANGEROUS

Your leadership style is an exact reflection of your perceptions, experiences and aspirations. On paper, my client – let's call him Simon – was an instrumental member of the leadership team. He always met objectives, usually well ahead of schedule. Yet he was the cause of the most significant issues the human resources department had to manage. While Simon was a gun at delivery, he left disaster in his wake. Staff morale was on the decline, bullying complaints began to pile up and staff absences became regular. Human resources soon assigned a business partner to assist with the increased work volume.

Simon was very much aware of the impact of his leadership style, acknowledging that his approach was not for everyone. When we worked together, he identified that his deliver-at-all-costs approach to leadership was instilled in him by his very first leader – someone who Simon saw as successful. This leader formed Simon's definition of leadership: the role of a leader was to know all of the answers, solve all of the problems and keep the caboose running at full speed. Followers were expected to execute commands. In the past, the wins outweighed the pain for his director. Then the pain exploded. Simon was no longer seen as the leader he aspired to be. His career stalled, almost coming to an end. Everything he had learnt and mastered was no longer effective.

Don't get me wrong – all learning is a journey of imitation. Many leaders are a fusion of their experiences and expectations of leadership. They have cherry-picked the attributes and styles of leaders they have admired and respected. However, you must evolve this and develop your own leadership style. You cannot be authentic when you are trying to imitate someone else.

As a leadership mentor, I mostly work with clients privately, one-on-one. Each client is like an old home under restoration. Just like removing the layers of wallpaper reflecting the trends of previous generations, the first step in enhancing their leadership impact and influence is to remove the layers of emulation.

Emulating others is exhausting. Another client, Mark, came to me and said he was tired of playing the role of leader. Where he lacked leadership capability, he imitated others. Mark spent his days swapping hats, unable to identify his authentic self as leader. His team told him they knew they weren't getting the real Mark. Mark felt the same way, but was unsure of how to get back from the ledge. I was able to help Mark identify his authentic leadership style.

After many years as a leader, you may be confused about your original wallpaper – who you are, as a leader, underneath all that reading, exposure, impression and imitation. It can be challenging to recognise the influences on your leadership style.

Activity: Mirror, mirror

Recognising the strengths and weaknesses of leaders you've encountered during your career may help you to understand their influences on your leadership style. Grab your journal, a pen and a cup of coffee and think about your last three leaders. Using their names as headings, answer the following questions:

· Describe their leadership style.

· What did you most admire about them?

· What about them frustrated you the most?

· What do you think prevented them from being more impactful?

· Can you recognise this leader's influence on your leadership style?

- Do the leadership attributes modelled by this leader align with your values? Are they congruent with the leadership legacy you hope to leave?

Be open to what may have contributed to your weaknesses as a leader. For some, this activity can feel like realising that you have become your mother or father. Eek!

TAKE YOUR BLINDERS OFF

Leading yourself is the foundation of impactful leadership. You will be the most complex person you will ever have to lead. In her research on self-awareness, Tasha Eurich, organisational psychologist, executive coach and author of *Insight: The Surprising Truth About How Others See Us, How We See Ourselves, and Why the Answers Matter More Than We Think*, found that 95 per cent of people think they are self-aware, but the actual number is less than 15 per cent. Eurich jokes that some 80 per cent of us are lying to ourselves about whether we are lying to ourselves. And that's on a good day! It is easy for us to see what needs improvement in others; it is far more difficult and requires a lot more observation to see what needs improvement in ourselves. This is all part of the human condition.

Many leaders wear 'cognitive blinders' that obscure their view of the world. This form of tunnel vision blocks out the potential for personal growth. You must remove your blinders.

There is a strong link between self-awareness and high performance. I have come to know that when you understand your internal state, you are simply more effective. Your internal state includes your strengths and weaknesses. If you are aware of your strengths and weaknesses, you have the opportunity to use your strengths intentionally, and optimise your weaknesses. Being aware of your weaknesses enables you to work more collabora- tively and effectively with others with differing strengths: you are able to easily recognise that someone else may have better ideas or abilities than your own. In my experience, when a leader becomes aware of their strengths and weaknesses, they take con- trol of the direction of their career.

I am often brought in to work with senior people leaders and tell them what everyone else is too afraid to say. Along the way, I have seen every reaction possible: long, awkward silences; shock; tears. Clients have stood up, gathered their belongings and stormed out of the room in a huff. There have been outbursts of anger. The emotional reaction is part of the journey. On the other side of a small amount of discomfort (and I get it, it may not seem small at the time) is an immense amount of power. Almost every leader I work with is devastated to learn of the unintended consequences of their impact. 'That was never my intention,' is usually the first thing that comes out of their mouths.

A client of mine – we'll call her Jane – serves as a case in point. Jane had repeatedly been given feedback that she speaks too often and for too long in meetings. When we first met, Jane told me that she wanted to improve this behaviour and learn how to be a more effective leader. Jane believed that she was being helpful. She did not see it coming when her team told her – out of frustration – that she was the reason they were unable to make better decisions. Upon reflection, Jane realised that she spent most meetings interjecting with her ideas, pro- viding extensive detail to ensure that she was understood. Jane thought others were silent because they were intimidated by her brilliance; she failed to read the room. She was unable to see that others were trying, without success, to speak. Eventually, her team concluded there was little benefit in having an opinion. It is one thing to be armed with the insight – the hardest part is knowing what to do next. This was where I helped Jane. The intention is to move from self-awareness to self-improvement.

There is a considerable amount of material on the topic of self-awareness. Every book, article, whitepaper, TED Talk, you name it, endorses the notion that self-awareness is the ability to see yourself clearly and objectively through reflection and introspection. But very few explain how to develop your self-awareness. I believe the best place to start is with a psychometric test, commonly known as a personality profile assessment. These tools help you understand your preferences, what you enjoy, things you dislike and what frustrates you. They also provide you with insight into how these attributes might show up for others, as well as their impact.

I use a psychometric test in almost all of my programs. The assessment platform I use is a fusion of many personality pro- filing frameworks; it allows me to help my clients understand their natural preferences. These preferences are what I like to call leadership motivators, which form the basis of our work- ing together. That is all. We do not dwell on the report, and I encourage you to do the same. See the report as a helpful and unbiased insight into parts of yourself that you need to see, even if it makes you feel a little uncomfortable at first.

The problem with these tools – and I must stress that they are just tools – is that people can get so hung up on the outcome. Humans are efficient beings. We like to put labels on things. It helps us make decisions more easily. Unfortunately, this leads to team members becoming pigeon-holed. Their personality profile becomes the validation for their behaviour or exclusion. Far too often, these tools become weapons, amplifying relation- ship issues. To avoid relationship breakdowns and frustration, consider these tools merely a window – a small view of a much larger picture. This view does not define who you are, who your team members are or what you can become.

Odds are that you will have undertaken one of these personality profile assessments at some point in your career, perhaps as part of a recruitment process. The endless list of questions might have seemed intent on catching you out. Questions such as, 'On a scale of 1 to 5, with 1 being strongly agree and 5 being strongly disagree, do you like to run with scissors?', are almost always followed up at around question number 258 with 'On a scale of 1 to 5, with 1 being strongly disagree and 5 being strongly agree, do you dislike running with scissors?' Psychometric tests use questions like these to prevent response bias and the possible distortion of results. It's like a check to see if you are awake and paying attention.

If you have never undertaken a personality profiling assessment before, or you were not provided with a profile debrief of an assessment you had completed, I strongly encourage you to sit one. There are more than two thousand different types of personality profile assessment tools, and it really doesn't matter which tool you choose – just pick one. The most popular is the Myers-Briggs Type Indicator, which is taken by more than two million people every year.

My favourite (and no, I am not affiliated) online assessment is 16personalities.com, based on the Myers-Briggs model. It provides an easy to read, beautifully illustrated free online report. Did I mention it was free? You can purchase a more detailed downloadable report if you want greater insight into your personality profile. Other frameworks include Strengths Finder, the Big Five, the Birkman Method and Enneagram. Google 'free personality test' and you will find many options.

Activity: Report reflection

Now what? How do you turn a report into a new you? Further along in this chapter, I introduce you to an activity called *You, unpacked*, which will help you establish a plan. For the time being, grab your personality profile report, your journal, a pen and a cup of coffee. Find yourself a quiet corner or a comfortable chair where you will not be interrupted. After reading your report, consider and make notes about the following:

· What stands out for you?
· What can you identify with?
· Does anything confuse you?
· What, if anything, invokes an emotional response?

Resist the urge to discount or justify. Keep in mind that the report is generic, based on what people who are *like* you have a preference for. Let's pretend, just for a moment, that the report has some truth. Consider the following:

· How could, or do, these preferences, attributes, behaviours, strengths or weaknesses show up?
· Can you identify these attributes in someone you work closely with? How do you experience these behaviours in them?

MAKE FRIENDS WITH FEEDBACK

Feedback is a great tool when used correctly. Unfortunately, it is often not as effective as possible because many of us do not know how to ask for feedback the right way. We don't know what we don't know, right? We are not taught the best way to elicit feedback. Instead, we ask broad questions – layered with desperation. Our colleagues, lost and unable to focus on any one matter, may provide a near-useless reply.

The interaction usually goes a little like this. After presenting to the group, Brenda asks her colleague, Susan, 'So, how did I go? I would love your feedback. You are always so honest.' Susan, not anticipating the request, quickly tries to recall the extensive presentation. After a little chuckle and a smirk, Susan tells Brenda, 'Well, it was good. You seemed very confident. Very detailed. And so many graphs. I am probably not the best person to ask about the impact of wage inflation on competing economies and scaled manufacturing, but I think others in the room seemed impressed. Great work!' Susan excuses herself in the hope of avoiding any detailed questioning. Brenda only hears that she is intelligent and very well prepared. Brenda had no idea what she wanted feedback on, and as a result, is none the wiser having received it.

This was a civilised example. I have witnessed the death of working relationships following the response to a request for feedback. Sometimes the giver sees it as an opportunity to let someone know what they really think about them. Other times, the receiver is so insulted by the feedback that they aggressively defend themselves.

Despite all your reflection about your personality assessment report, you may be no more the wiser. If that is the case, you need to call for backup. By backup I mean a friend, colleague or mentor to help provide you with some feedback. Sometimes you are too close to the problem – you! A friend, colleague or mentor can help provide you with the guidance you need to see yourself without bias.

There is an art to the solicitation and filtering of feedback. It helps if you are specific about the feedback you are seeking. It is just as important to select the right people to provide this feedback. Use the 'Ten steps to powerful feedback' and the sample script below to ask the right people the right questions.

If you think people might be hesitant to share their thoughts, allow them to do so anonymously. HR or even a trusted colleague may be able to facilitate this. You often learn the most from what people are afraid to tell you.

Ten steps to powerful feedback

1. **Be specific.** What exactly do you want feedback on? Using Brenda from the above example, did she want feedback on her content, stage presence or ability to engage and influence her audience?

2. **Be clear about why you are seeking feedback.** You may be wanting to improve your ability to engage and influence others because you realise communication is currently a weakness. You might have to make an important presentation, and you want to make sure that the audience can take action. Being clear about why you are seeking feedback provides your colleagues with context.

3. **Identify colleagues you wish to receive feedback from.** Be specific about the reason for their selection. Do you believe that they possess the skill you feel you are lacking? Has someone suggested you connect with them because they have many years of experience that you could benefit from? If they are not someone you feel you can learn from, keep looking. To get the most out of feedback, seek diversity of opinion, background and personality type.

4. **Invite your colleagues to provide you with feedback.** If you're unsure how to word the request, use the feedback request script I have provided later in this chapter. Provide your colleagues with adequate time to prepare. Brenda should have approached Susan before her presentation to ensure she was ready and focused on providing detailed and valuable feedback. Susan may have been

able to recommend a different colleague Brenda might not have considered. Never surprise someone with a request for feedback. Be gracious and understanding if they elect not to participate.

5. **Make a time to meet with each colleague independently to hear and discuss their feedback.** Allow them the time to digest and consider their feedback.

6. **Be open to feedback.** Be ready to hear it. Others will be sharing their opinions, insights and perceptions of you. It is common to feel apprehensive. Expect those providing you with feedback to also feel apprehensive. Be in a relaxed mood when you meet to receive feedback.

7. **Listen.** The feedback you receive may anger or sadden you. Do not interrupt the person giving you feedback. Do not discount their opinion or defend yourself. Your job is to listen. When you listen, your mouth should be closed.

8. **Thank the feedback giver.** Do so genuinely.

9. **Tell the feedback giver what you intend to do with the feedback.** It may well be that you intend, at least initially, to simply reflect on their advice. That is perfectly okay. When you have finished your reflection, follow up and let them know what you intend to do. Hopefully, their feedback was delivered with the best of intentions. If you do not intend to take any of their advice on board, you can still thank them for opening your eyes to new possibilities in developing your leadership skills.

10. **Take action.** Commit to the change that is required. It may be small. It may take a lifetime. Keep the dialogue open with the person who provided you with feedback. Make the journey of growth visible – givers of feedback like to see how you get on. Let them know how your next presentation, for example, went. What did you take on board and what was the result? Developing relationships like these deepen your network and may prove to be invaluable in the future.

Feedback request script

The following script shows how Brenda should have invited Susan to provide feedback. Use it as a guide for your own feedback requests. This conversation can happen via an in-person chat or an email – it all depends on the relationship you have with your colleagues.

Hi Susan,

I have been focusing on improving my presentation skills. In particular, I would like to ensure that I can engage my audience with relevant and exciting information. I have been invited to be the keynote speaker at the National Conference in November – the first time I have been invited to speak at such a large event. I was in the room last year when you spoke at the Global Corporate Services Conference and was very impressed with your in-depth knowledge of emerging trends and your ability to keep everyone in the room engaged. I learnt a lot about something I had previously known very little about. I have been invited to deliver a short speech summarising my topic on Thursday, at the Monthly Executive Forum. I believe you are exceptionally skilled at public speaking, and I would value your feedback on my summary speech. If it is convenient for you, perhaps we could meet for coffee on the following Monday.

Kind regards,

Brenda

IF YOU CAN'T CHANGE IT, EMBRACE IT

You cannot be an authentic leader if you hide your flaws. You are less likely to be influential wearing a metaphorical mask. Leadership development programs innately focus on 'fixing' personality issues, but suppression is futile. They key is to acknowledge your leadership shortcomings and, where change is not possible, embrace them. You and your personality traits are like a volume knob. You need to know when to turn it up and when to turn it down. But it is not a mute button.

Just because someone gives you negative feedback does not necessarily mean you must hide or change that attribute.

I am not talking about destructive behaviours here. Abuse in the workplace is never okay. I have experienced the effects of abuse and toxic cultures firsthand. Toxic leaders can destroy people. There are never any winners, and the consequences are lasting.

You may have spent much of your career focusing on abolishing a perceived negative attribute. It might be a challenge to see an opportunity to leverage it. Yet, here I am, suggesting you embrace this something – and that, by doing so, you will be more successful.

I am impatient. Very impatient. In my first role as a leader, I was focused on efficiency. I wanted to prove myself and show that I could lead a team to greatness. This passion for efficiency clashed with some of my team members. I was not aware of their feelings, and I had not considered how I might be perceived. I just wanted everyone to get on with things. I believed they had lost too much time in discussion, and it was up to me to get them back on track. But no matter what I did, or how I sold it, I was met with iron-fisted resistance. Repetition and demands did not seem to work.

As a new leader, lost and confused, and without any leadership training, I approached a director in my office. He was someone I respected and felt comfortable being open with. He removed my blinders and expanded my worldview. Our discussions provided me with valuable insight into how I was perceived. It was never my intention to frustrate or offend anyone; however, my impatience had a negative, unintended impact. I was able to reflect and engage with my team more effectively. Did it teach me patience? Nope. It did, however, give me the power to understand this weakness. I learnt to allow others the time and the space to discover and accept. I learnt to delegate tasks to those in the team who had a tremendous passion and skill for detail. I did not eliminate what I perceived to be a negative trait. When leveraged, my impatience is decisiveness. I can navigate complexity very quickly.

As a result of my new approach, my team perceived that I had become more patient. All I did was adjust the volume knob. Find relief in knowing that you do not need to change who you are.

Activity: You, unpacked

Grab your notes from your review of your personality report, which you compiled in the previous activity: report reflection. Identify any traits, attributes or behaviours that emerged. For example, let's say you identified that you are impatient, funny and visionary. Using the analysis template below, sort your identified traits, behaviours or attributes as either a strength or a weakness and list them under the respective 'me' column.

For each trait, behaviour or attribute, whether it be a strength or a weakness, think about what it looks like when it is amplified. By amplified, I mean if the volume is cranked up high. What does it look like when, good or bad, this strength is seen as a weakness and vice versa? Could there be a negative slant to your perceived strength? Conversely, how could your weaknesses be seen as positives? There are no right or wrong answers.

Finally, think about what your focus needs to be to ensure that your strengths are intentional, and you leverage any weaknesses. For example, I consider humour a strength. But, when it's amplified as a weakness, humour can be perceived as immaturity – and leaders using it can be seen as irresponsible. My focus, therefore, is to be mindful and use humour appropriately.

Be aware that your strengths can derail you just as much as your weaknesses can. If you are lost, ask a trusted colleague or friend – someone who knows you well. Tell them that you have always seen [insert trait, behaviour or attribute] in a negative light. Ask them, 'Can you see how this trait may benefit me if I decided to use it for good?'

Be open to consider how a negative trait, leveraged, might be your superpower. A leader's superpower is their most positive and impactful personality trait – something that enhances their influence. Your superpower, while an extraordinary ability, will be second nature to you. Whether you were born with it or developed it over time, you may have, until now, undervalued it. You know you have found your superpower when you can't articulate exactly how you do it.

Strength/weakness analysis template

Strength		
Me	**Amplified as a weakness**	**Focus**
Funny	Irresponsible	Be sure to use humour appropriately. Consider the feelings of others in a situation.
Visionary	Foolish, unrealistic	Translate the vision for the future. Relate it to where we are now. What is the next step? Tell the story of the journey.

Me	Amplified as a strength	Focus
		Weakness
Impatient	Decisive	Communicate regularly. Articulate the need for urgency. Delegate where necessary.

EMOTIONAL MASTERY

Managing your emotions is essential. With hindsight, most of the bad decisions people make are impulsive and bring waves of shame, resentment and anger. The inability to manage potent negative emotions can bring an end to even the most enduring careers in a fleeting moment. Leaders who can self-regulate have a more significant impact and stay in leadership roles longer. By self-regulate, I mean the ability to control your emotions, behaviour and thoughts in the pursuit of a long-term goal. While an outburst may address an immediate perceived issue, it could derail your long-term plans. The ability to self-regulate is your ability to dial character traits up and down according to the situation.

> *I've never seen the tendency toward radical outbursts to surface as an indicator of strong leadership.*
>
> – Daniel Goleman

Mastering your emotions does not mean suppressing them. This is only a disaster waiting to happen. Emotions are all part of the human condition. By mastering your emotions, I mean understanding and leveraging them – channelling them into something productive rather than destructive.

Impulses drive your emotions. You will respond to your environment, experiences and interactions with others with a feeling. Being around friends, for example, brings feelings of happiness – just as working with a particular colleague incites feelings of frustration. We all feel these emotions. It is a long-standing myth that negative emotions result in adverse outcomes. Research published in the *Academy of Management Journal* suggests that emotions can support decision-making performance. Leaders who can identify and control the impact of bias from their feelings achieve higher, positively sustainable decision-making performance.

Emotions are not just about crying. While sadness is a valid feeling, most leaders hear the word 'emotions' and instantly associate it with tears. Emotions can range from anger, distress, irritability, misery, nervousness and disenchantment to gladness, happiness, bliss, excitement, appreciation and contentment.

Think about your last emotional reaction – positive or negative, it doesn't matter. What did you feel at that particular moment? What was your reaction? Consider what may have triggered that response. Have you responded this way before? Is there a pattern? Replay the situation in your mind, in slow motion and from the perspective of a fly on the wall. What really happened?

At first, it can be challenging to identify the trigger while we are in the moment. Identify the feeling. Label it. Is it anger, frustration, sadness, or happiness? What immediately preceded this feeling?

Avoid resigning yourself to particular behaviours. Mastering your emotions takes time.

FROM SELF-AWARENESS TO
SELF-IMPROVEMENT

There is little benefit to having all this insight into who you are if you do nothing with it. Your focus as an impactful leader is to grow every day. Vulnerability can be hard. Be open to considering your true strengths and weaknesses. What gaps exist between your current state and where you aspire to be? What is the best thing to do to move closer to this aspiration?

Your leadership journey needn't be lonely. Share your journey with others. Invite them in. Listen to their war stories. It can be hard to be vulnerable, but it is harder to take action. There are people less qualified than you who are much further ahead simply because they took action.

CONCLUSION

Leaders are human. We also carry a lot of responsibility. To be successful, it is useful to be aware of yourself – your strengths, weaknesses and emotions. You need to be able to self-regulate and be mindful of your impact on others.

Thinking about who you are, what you value and how you show up can be challenging. Looking in a mirror can be uncomfortable. But insight is a gift. Commit to being challenged with compassionate confrontation to identify your core strengths and leadership weaknesses. Leadership weaknesses plague your success, render you ineffective and have the potential to damage credibility.

In the next chapter, you will work out what motivates the team that you lead.

2

Understanding others

*Before you are a leader, success is all about growing
yourself. When you become a leader, success is all about
growing others.*

– Jack Welch, former chairman and CEO of General Electric

There is no 'I' in 'team'. (Insert eye roll.) Cheesy statements do
my head in, but this one, as it turns out, happens to be very
accurate. The best leaders see success as a group endeavour.
Understanding how and what motivates your people is the key
to unlocking their potential. Leadership is no different to any
other interaction. Along the way, you will meet people who are
very similar to you. You'll easily relate to them and establish a
relationship. Others, on the other hand, may confront you,
making even the simplest of interactions tense and strained.
You may struggle to understand why they act the way they
do, leading to frustration, withdrawal and, at times, anger.
These experiences shape future interactions, creating a cycle of
diminishing connection.

In chapter 1, I highlighted the value of being introspective. You identified your strengths and weaknesses. More importantly, you learnt how to adjust the volume knob of these attributes to ensure you are intentional at your best and leveraged when you may be at your worst. I am not talking about toxic behaviours, which are never okay. Harmful personality traits do not result in impactful leadership. I have experienced toxic leadership first-hand, and I am on a mission to eradicate these behaviours in the workplace.

Understanding others is not much different to the process of understanding yourself. When you have a strong awareness of self – married with an understanding of others – you generate trust. Trust is invaluable in leadership. It drives relationships.

The future of leadership development, I am certain, will be heavily focused on the building of trust.

Over two years, Google's people operations department interviewed more than 200 employees in a quest to unlock the secret of effective teams. Their research found the composition of the team itself was not as important as anticipated. Members and their expertise mattered less than how members of the group interacted, structured their work and viewed their contributions. Google identified five fundamental dynamics that set successful teams apart from others. The most critical was psychological safety – in other words, trust. The remaining four attributes were dependability; structure and clarity; meaning of work; and impact of work.

For almost 25 years, global business media organisation Fortune has partnered with Great Place to Work, an agency committed to enhancing company cultures, to produce the

100 Best Companies to Work For. This annual list, much like the Fortune 500, consistently demonstrates that trust between managers and employees is the primary defining characteristic of the very best workplaces.

To reap the rewards of trust, you must first unlock the mystery of understanding others. One of the reasons leaders earn the big bucks is that they must manage diverse people. Steven J Stowell, co-founder of the Center for Management and Organization Effectiveness, said, 'Great leaders find ways to connect with their people and help them fulfil their potential.'

CHILDREN, ANIMALS AND EMPLOYEES

WC Fields was an American comedian, actor and writer. His comic persona was a sarcastic egotist who had contempt for many things. Fields was best known for his saying, 'Never work with animals or children' – alluding to their unpredictable behaviour on the stage and movie sets. At times, I wonder if the adage is incomplete. Perhaps 'Never work with animals, children or employees' is more appropriate? My intention is not to be derogatory. I do not believe employees are immature animals. I am merely acknowledging the challenges all leaders face at times when leading others. On occasion, it can seem that your team members, the people who are supposed to be on the same side as you, can be just as unpredictable as children and animals. There are no user manuals.

In chapter 1, I highlighted the benefits of using personality profiling tools. These provide an unbiased insight into the personality preferences of people who are like you. I encouraged you to sit one, to learn whether or not you are effective at playing to your strengths and leveraging your weaknesses.

In a team setting, my advice is very different. When used effectively, personality profiling can assist in raising group awareness of preferences and motivators within the team to support the journey to high performance. However, personality profiling is often thrust upon a group by a leader who has very little insight into their leadership effectiveness. Rather than being used to celebrate members of the team and what they bring, confused leaders deploy these assessments in the hope of discovering the operating manual for each of their staff members. You might like to heed my advice: the absence of transparency about why you wish to implement such a tool and what you intend to do with it will only accelerate the death of team morale. Only use psychometric tests in your team to encourage more effective collaboration.

WITS' END

'These people are a nightmare!' Brett screamed down the phone to me. 'I need them to step up. I left an amazing job, working with a high-performing team,' he said. It was a Saturday evening, and Brett had spent Friday night and all day Saturday redoing his team's work to meet a Monday deadline. 'I have tried to inspire them. I have tried to empower them. I am now resorting to threats of performance management. They are unwavering. It is as if they are actively resisting me,' he conceded in defeat.

I first met Brett at one of my public workshops. I learnt from my chat with Brett that he had come from an operational role where he had developed a strong reputation for exceeding targets. His technical skills were highly prized. He told me about how he had struggled to advance his career and move into a leadership role. Though often landing an interview, Brett would not make it to the next round. In almost all instances, he fell short due to his apparent lack of people-engagement skills.

Brett quickly followed with his favourite Steve Jobs quote: 'If you want to make everyone happy, don't be a leader – sell ice cream.'

What struck me was Brett's interpretation of this quote. I don't think Jobs intended to imply that leaders should disregard others' happiness. Instead, he was saying that a leadership role requires a clear vision, supported by laser-like focus, to achieve objectives. You cannot be all things to all people. Jobs, contrary to Brett's interpretation, invested heavily in people. The cry of the ignorant leader seeks to impose their authority. 'I'm leading, and people will follow. They have a choice – they are either on or off the bus.'

The number of buses that appear in leadership stories is always amusing, but I digress. You might relate to Brett's experience. Leadership frustration is common, but impactful leaders know how to navigate these challenges and, as they say, turn the ship around.

SOFT AND FLUFFY

Harvard University, the Carnegie Foundation and Stanford Research Center have unanimously concluded that 85 per cent of business success rests on people skills (soft skills). Technical skills (hard skills) and other abilities contribute only 15 per cent. This is not new information. For more than a century, we have known that people skills are more critical to organisational success than technical ability. These findings were based on the 1918 research and published works of Charles Riborg Mann, a physicist, engineer and civilian adviser in the United States War Department. Astonishingly, less than 30 per cent of the $510 billion invested by organisations globally on leadership development is spent on people skills, according to the American Society of Training and Development.

Back to my client, Brett. Brett had developed impressive hard skills. Hard skills are your expertise or technical capabilities – developed through experience, education or specific training. The skills I leveraged when I was providing advice as an accountant were my hard skills. Unfortunately for Brett, he had little to no soft skills. Soft skills are more challenging to measure. Compared with your technical skills, they can seem somewhat fluffy. You call upon your soft skills when, for example, you confront a challenging situation or need to have a courageous conversation. Unlike hard skills, soft skills are transferable across sectors and occupations. The list of these skills seems to evolve, which only makes it more challenging to master. Researchers, however, agree that soft skills include traits such as:

- communication
- empathy
- integrity
- dependability
- self-motivation
- teamwork
- creativity
- critical thinking
- adaptability
- the ability to work under pressure.

Australian workplace learning and recognition organisation DeakinCo. anticipates that by 2030, 63 per cent of all jobs will be soft-skill intensive. This is a significant shift in the structure of the global workforce. DeakinCo. found the demand for these skills outstrips supply by a staggering 45 per cent. Despite soft skills being nine times more potent than hard skills, DeakinCo.'s research indicated less than 1 per cent of Australian employees claim to have these skills in their LinkedIn profiles.

If these are not good enough reasons to consider developing your people skills to remain competitive, keep in mind soft skills cannot be reliably automated. Artificial intelligence can replicate hard skills at greater accuracy and speed and significantly lower cost. Robots, so far, have been unable to replicate the human condition. It is impossible to create an algorithm for soft skills.

Rest assured that there is nothing soft about soft skills.

THE POWER OF EMPATHY

There is nothing like life experience. Time is a great teacher, but our life experiences can be incredibly diverse. Without actually living other's lives, how exactly can you understand them? How do you connect with others and build trust at the same time? The secret is empathy. Empathy is the experience of understanding another person's thoughts, feelings and condition from his or her point of view, perspective and reality – rather than your own. Empathy is, metaphorically speaking, stepping into someone else's shoes or seeing things through someone else's eyes. Empathy is the oil that keeps relationships running smoothly.

I was a leader of people before I was 30 years old. My journey towards insight and growth was rocky and, at times, scary. I was fortunate enough to find someone willing to be my mentor – someone who gifted me time and saw what I could not see in myself. Best of all, he agreed to do it for free! One of the many things he taught me was that to be successful, I needed to show empathy. I cringed, fearful that I would now have to pander to my team. I did not share their life experiences. How could I possibly put myself in their shoes?

Many leaders become paralysed by the process of engaging with their team. In an attempt to show empathy, they pander. Their pandering is insincere and driven by fear – they retreat at the sheer thought of engaging in an awkward conversation. This is not empathy. You need not feign interest, understanding or emotion. There is no prerequisite of having lived a similar experience to empathise with someone. You need only to be present and listen. Consider how their perception or experience might impact them. Understanding others does not imply your agreement with their feelings or point of view. Instead, empathy means that you recognise their point of view and accept that it is different from yours.

I consider myself a great problem-solver – well, that's what I'd like people to think about me. It is a good skill to have. However, I have had to learn to resist the temptation to fix things. I would always jump into solution mode. A team member would come to me with a problem, and as they were talking, I would be nodding, all the while formulating a plan of attack. I was not listening. Instead, I was looking for a solution. I would convince myself that my intentions were good, despite their anger. Without using these exact words, I was telling them to get over it. It was not my intention to discount their perceptions and feelings. I did not see things through their eyes – this limited engagement and relationships with my staff.

Eventually, I realised that – unless they specifically asked for a solution – all my team members wanted was to be heard and acknowledged. They wanted validation. In most instances, the act of just listening was enough to help them take the next step themselves. I quickly gained a greater understanding of their values, aspirations and motivations. I was able to align them more appropriately with particular tasks and opportunities.

My team members soon began to share ideas and collaborate more effectively. Innovation flowed. I had developed a highly engaged and happy team. It felt as though I had acquired some form of leadership superpower. A happy team will self-manage. Leaders can step back from operational matters, genuinely delegate and empower others – all the while focusing on accelerating not only the organisational objectives but those established internally to enhance the customer experience.

CONNECTION

When starting in a new leadership role, the fastest way to demonstrate empathy is to meet with each team member one-on-one. Informal, private chats are a great way to get to know each other and for your team members to ask you any questions they may have. Team members will always have lots of questions for a newly appointed leader. This chat is best held away from the office – perhaps at a cafe. I tell them a little about myself. I share why I was interested in the role and provide insight into my aspirations for our shared future. I also share what I know of how senior management would like to see our team grow. It provides both a level of urgency and an endorsement to any change agenda I may have. I usually frame it like this: 'One of the reasons I got the role was my previous experience with [insert project, change agenda or new initiative]. This is something the organisation is keen to see our team develop.' Link this back to your aspirations of a shared future.

I then invite my team members to tell me a little about themselves, their role and what they enjoy about it, and what they consider as opportunities for improvement within the team.

Most people enjoy talking about themselves, as well as sharing their opinions. You will learn more about your team members in these one-on-one chats than any personality profiling assessment could provide. During your chat, don't just listen to what they say, but also how they say it. Be aware of body language and emotions.

Finally, open the floor. Invite them to ask you anything they like. Assure them that if it is inappropriate or something that you cannot share at this point, you will let them know. If it is something that you cannot discuss, explain to them why. It might be personal, and too soon in your working relationship to talk about it. If it relates to a confidential matter such as performance management, be very clear about the personal nature of the issue. If there will be an opportunity to discuss these matters in the future, share that with them. You want to show that you are both transparent and responsible.

If you are an established leader, developing and showing more empathy is a little more complicated. There is nothing more painful than an ill-prepared but highly energised people leader who has returned from a full-day masterclass, eager to try out their newfound skill. To be effective, share your story of insight. You will need to be vulnerable here. Link it with a review and feedback process. Perhaps it was your annual performance review or a peer feedback activity. Share with your team the realisation that you made, which will enhance team culture and performance. Do not skip the vital step of setting the scene. Otherwise, your team will be confused.

It is essential to maintain regular, informal dialogue with your team members. Do not solely focus on your direct reports. Build a relationship with each member of your team.

Nine steps to build empathy

1. **Put aside your viewpoint.** Try to see things as others see them. You may understand more clearly why they are reacting the way they are.

2. **Acknowledge and validate their perspective.** Acknowledgement does not necessarily mean that you agree with their feelings or point of view. Remember – in this process, your feelings and point of view are irrelevant.

3. **Listen deeply.** Put your complete focus on the person in front of you without becoming distracted. Your only job is to listen. Do not attempt to convey the thoughts, beliefs, values, assumptions or feelings of others.

4. **Provide encouragement.** When they have finished speaking, your contribution to the conversation should be of encouragement. Unless you were invited, do not share what you would do if you were in their position. Again, this interaction is not about you.

5. **Communicate your understanding.** If you are stuck on how to empathise, simply say, 'I can see how you may feel this way' – a neutral opener.

6. **Drive the conversation gently.** The focus should be on moving forward at a pace that is comfortable for them. Ask, 'What do you intend to do next?'. If they appear stumped, ask them, 'What would you suggest someone in a similar situation should do?' Though their response may not align with your own opinion, they will easily find a solution aligned with theirs.

7. **Offer support.** Ask if there is anything you can do. Do not pander and, again, do not attempt to fix. This process can be complex, and you might feel stuck. Trust me. They will find their way through this.

8. **Allow breathing space.** After your conversation, encourage them to get some fresh air – take a walk or grab a coffee. Invite them to get in touch with you if they need anything further.

9. **Do not be surprised if they thank you for your support.** You may feel that you have provided very little, but your puzzling response of 'Really?' does not instil confidence. Respond with, 'Always happy to help!'

CONCLUSION

Right now, you might be thinking that this is all too hard. The process of building awareness of others, their perceptions and their feelings can be daunting. Rest assured that it does get easier with time. As you become more in tune with your people, you will reap the benefits of increased loyalty, heightened engagement, improved teamwork, increased creativity and happier team members. You, too, will be happier as a result!

In the next chapter, you will learn how to bring the two lenses of awareness – awareness of self and awareness of others – together.

3

But, why?

Where there is no vision, the people perish.

– Proverbs 29:18

I once read somewhere that, on average, a child asks more than 100 questions per hour. 'Why? Why? But why?' my four-year-old daughter, Olivia, will ask. She is a curious and spirited individual who – like most children – asks 'why' repeatedly to the point of annoyance. You might be able to relate. In frustration, having exhausted every possible avenue of explanation, you snap, 'Just because!' Why do we stop asking the most critical question – 'Why?'

As a leader, you are tasked with inspiring others to action. I do not mean for you to bore them to death with vision and mission statements. During my career in the public sector, no year was complete without the obligatory – and, may I add, painful – process of revisiting our vision, mission and values. Despite the considerable cost of futurists and facilitators, we always seemed to end up with a slightly tweaked version of what we already had. My favourite tweak was the evolution of 'with passion' to 'with a service heart'. Profound!

It reminds me of a funny story – and by funny, I mean ridiculous. I once worked for a CEO obsessed with the purpose statement of a company that made airbags. As an organisation, we had no connection with the automotive industry, yet he was captivated by the simplicity of 'We save lives'. It consumed his entire thought process. Some two years later, he was no closer to articulating his leadership purpose. As a result, organisational performance and growth came to a grinding halt. You cannot manufacture your purpose.

The Business Case for Purpose, published by Harvard Business Review, suggests that almost half of all employees report a disconnection between senior leadership over purpose. Though sectors, products and services may be vastly different, sweeping purpose statements in organisations from all corners of the globe share very similar themes. Think about those motivational posters that (hopefully used to) litter the walls – a generic value in large capital letters, complemented by some aspirational waffle, all under an imposing photograph of a soaring eagle or proud lion. This chapter is not about organisational visions and missions, nor about rah-rah speeches and pep talks. As you exhale in relief, take those posters down. It is no longer 1993.

A 2020 Gallup poll found that a dismal 22 per cent of employees are actively engaged at work. Actively engaged employees are passionate about their work and have an emotional attachment to their team and organisation. Engaged team members are creative and high performing, delivering above and beyond the requirements of their job for the organisation's benefit. That leaves a whopping 78 per cent of employees who are not engaged or are actively disengaged at work. Actively disengaged employees are unhappy, resentful and spread negativity. Despite rarely delivering to expectation, they outlast actively engaged team members. Recognise anyone?

Impactful leaders need enthusiastic followers who follow not because they have to, but because they want to.

Simon Sinek became fascinated by the great leaders of the world and sought to help people become more inspired at work – and, in turn, inspire their colleagues. His 2009 TED Talk, viewed more than 55 million times, popularised the concept of *why*. Sinek was curious about why some leaders were more innovative, more influential and more successful than others. More importantly, he was interested in why very few of these successful leaders could repeat their success across different projects, teams and organisations. Having spent many years studying the behaviour of leaders, Sinek realised that great leaders inspire action by promoting *why* they do something, not *what* they do. Put simply, *why* means purpose – your reason for being.

Purpose, as a notion, is not new. For centuries, the Japanese have appreciated the benefit of finding meaning in life. Known as *ikigai* (pronounced 'eye-ka-guy'), your reason for being is linked to longevity. Dan Buettner, American National Geographic explorer and author of *The Blue Zones: Lessons on Living Longer from the People Who've Lived the Longest*, studied areas in the world that were home to the longest-living residents. Buettner concluded that having one thing that keeps you interested, focused and provides a sense of personal satisfaction may lead to a longer and happier life. In recent times, the *people* people (human resource academics and professionals) have coined the term 'meaningful work'.

In chapter 2 I mentioned the quest Google's people operations department embarked upon to find the secret to high-performing teams. Of the five fundamental dynamics that set successful teams apart from others, Google identified *meaning* as the fourth most critical attribute. Google defined meaning as something personally significant. I love the idea of meaningful work as a source of personal growth, shared purpose and inspiration. I will use *why*, purpose, meaning and meaningful interchangeably. What you call it is not important. For simplicity, let's define it as what gets you up every morning and keeps you going.

THE POWER OF *WHY*

According to LinkedIn, purpose-oriented employees have higher levels of engagement and fulfilment with their work. They outperform their peers in every indicator, including expected tenure and leadership competencies. Connecting your employees to purpose brings tangible business impact. Global peer coaching platform Imperative found that purpose-oriented employees had 64 per cent higher levels of fulfilment in their work; were 50 per cent more likely to be in leadership roles; and were 47 per cent more likely to promote their employers. The plethora of studies on engagement demonstrates that, on average, organisations with highly engaged employees experience 40 per cent less turnover than organisations with low employee engagement – and 22 per cent higher productivity.

The Business Case for Purpose, published by Harvard Business Review, found 89 per cent of the executives surveyed agreed that purpose was essential in driving performance. Almost unanimously, 474 global executives endorsed the notion that organisations with shared purpose have higher employee satisfaction. Disappointingly, less than half of those surveyed indicated their organisation had a strong sense of shared purpose. Harvard Business School, in a similar study, found that fewer than 20 per cent of leaders have a strong sense of their purpose.

The days of carrot and stick, or commander and follower, have gone. Purpose and meaning provide motivation and inspiration.

The workplace is in the midst of an immense generational shift. Millennials – those born between 1981 and 1996 – are intent on developing purpose-driven careers. According to Gallup, 71 per cent of millennials who align with the purpose of their organisation and leader plan to stay for at least a year. While this may not sound like a raving endorsement of purpose-driven leadership, bear in mind that millennials do not see loyalty with an employer the same way baby boomers did. Just 54 per cent of millennials, at the time of the study, were in full-time employment. While this generation is experiencing the impact of horrific economic turbulence, resulting in high levels of both unemployment and underemployment, flexibility is highly valued. As countries begin to win the battle against the COVID-19 pandemic and economies start to return to 'normal', businesses large and small will have to adapt to this working preference. A significant change in the composition of our workforce requires a unique leadership skill.

Those leaders who possess the capability of processing their life and work experiences into wisdom – and ultimately a sense of purpose – are the most equipped and inspiring leaders to follow in this complex and volatile digital world.

– Jonathan Donner, former head of executive development at Amazon and Unilever

Have you ever experienced someone who had a passion so intense it oozed from their pores? Perhaps they were a leader. Maybe they were a motivational speaker, a celebrity, an athlete or an activist. Regardless of what they did, their enthusiasm was magnetic – inspirational, you might say. They pulled you into their purpose. When you engage in dialogue about your purpose, you stimulate reflection in others and find common ground. What many refer to as purpose naturally rises to the top. Sinek says, 'We want to be around people and organizations who are like us and share our beliefs.' Genuine collaboration is not possible without a purpose.

On the flip side, have you ever worked for a leader who talks endlessly about empowerment? This buzzword is often sprinkled into pep talks when productivity and accountability have taken a dive. It is usually the hallmark of a leader without a purpose – someone who spruiks empowerment to divert attention from their lack of competency, passing the buck of goalsetting on to their team. Despite their enthusiasm, they probably don't know what empowerment looks like. When leaders rely on empowerment, expectations and boundaries are often not established. Staff interpret this newly formed corporate value as an order to go forth and accomplish. Extremes start to emerge, and empowerment is construed as authority. A little too late, the CEO realises a mistake has been made. Innovation and accountability come to an abrupt end, causing confusion and disappointment.

Purpose turns potential into performance.

A highly developed purpose, however, is the compass by which your people can navigate. The great news is that you do not have to be the CEO to be a visionary leader! Leaders who are driven by a strong sense of purpose spur innovation and transformational change. They inspire and engage followers to shift focus from short-term delivery to long-term value creation. Purpose turns potential into performance. Harvard Business School professor Rebecca Henderson said, 'The sense of being part of something greater than yourself can lead to high levels of engagement, high levels of creativity, and the willingness to partner.'

It may come as a surprise that purpose does not just trickle down automatically. How can this be true when we spend considerable time cascading organisational objectives to directorates, departments, teams and individuals? These objectives are merely intended outcomes. *Why* ties it all together.

DRIVEN BY A CAUSE

It has become the stuff of legend. As with all fables, the sequence of events may differ – yet the underlying moral remains. During a tour of NASA headquarters in 1962, President John F Kennedy encountered a janitor mopping the floors. Some say that the president broke away from the tour to engage with the janitor. Others suggest the president asked the janitor why he was working so late. From my studies of Kennedy's leadership style, I like to believe that he saw more in the power of connecting with people and lost interest in the tour itself.

However you imagine the story goes, the president introduced himself and expressed interest in what the janitor was doing. 'Mr President,' the janitor responded, 'I'm helping put a man on the moon.' Rather than saying, 'I'm mopping floors,' the janitor identified that his work directly supported the purpose of putting a man on the moon. More than 50 years ago, when

Neil Armstrong took 'one giant leap for mankind', it was the last step in a process that captivated the hearts, minds and purpose of the more than 400,000 employees and contractors working at NASA. Fact or fiction, this example demonstrates the power of singularity of purpose.

Shared goals are not always shared outcomes. Your intended outcomes may not be aligned with those of your team members, or may even be in sharp contrast – despite sharing a goal. There was a time in my career when I wanted to demonstrate my capability in formulating and implementing a transformation strategy. However, my team members were focused on making their jobs easier, and my vision only sounded like more work. Our intended outcomes were different, yet we had a shared goal – that our services and customer experience added value and not noise, with reduced effort. My job was to unite our aspirations to drive collaboration.

With your newfound understanding of your team members and their motivations, consider what their aspirations might be. Is there an underlying purpose or 'goal' that can unite their aspirations with yours?

YOUR *WHY* INSPIRES ACTION

Contrary to popular belief, you do not just find your *why*. It is not misplaced in the back of a drawer. You must build your *why*, working at it over time. Your *why* is you at your best – capturing your lived experience, values, aspirations and passions. Articulating this, however, can be like answering, 'How do you breathe?' I like to keep things simple. When working with clients, I ask them to complete the following activity.

Activity: Why, oh why?

Grab your journal, a pen and a cup of coffee and find yourself a quiet corner to ponder the following questions:

· What lights you up? What provokes excitement or passion in you?

· How would you describe your authentic self, with all pretence stripped away?

· What is important to you?

· What creates a sense of motivation in you?

· What are your innate strengths? What do people come to you for?

· How do you add value?

· How does this relate to those you work with?

Sometimes others see in us what we cannot see in ourselves. Find at least three people you trust who have chosen to be connected with you – not a family member who is forced to love you. Explain to them that you are refining your purpose in leadership and would like to understand the value you bring to the people you care about. Using the questions above as a guide, ask them:

· What do you think I am passionate about?

· When I am authentically myself, what do I bring to our relationship?

· What do you most admire about me?

· How do I inspire or motivate you?

· What do you value in me? What can I do that you cannot?

· Why are you friends with me?

How do the responses from those in your personal and professional network compare to your own? Does this provide insight into your purpose? Is your purpose more than your current job description?

Remember, your *why* will not magically crystalise overnight. Articulating your purpose takes reflection. The most significant benefit of a well-defined purpose is the depth and emotional connection that it brings to storytelling. Storytelling, which we will discuss in chapter 6, is the unfair leadership advantage.

CONCLUSION

In part I, I discussed the importance of leading yourself before leading others. You learnt how to be intentional with your strengths while leveraging your weaknesses. You discovered there are more perspectives of the world than your own and that, by showing empathy, you can build a deep relationship with your team. In this chapter, you discovered how a strong *why* can leverage trust to build morale and personal accomplishment.

In part II, I will show you how to build leadership clarity – a valuable skill to bring people along on a journey scattered with ambiguity.

LEADERSHIP CLARITY

4

There's more certainty than you think

The leader is one who, out of the clutter, brings simplicity … out of discord, harmony … and out of difficulty, opportunity.

– Albert Einstein

Humans are interesting beings. We hunger for certainty. We know that it is impossible to tell what the future will bring, yet we want assurance. Not knowing what to do or what will happen breeds worry and anxiety. Our ability to deal with this is dependent upon our ability to tolerate uncertainty.

As a leader, it is helpful to be highly tolerant. You might be familiar with the studies showing that people would rather experience the certainty of an electric shock over the possibility of one: even when the possibility of an electric shock was extremely low, stress levels in study participants were high. It is only natural that, in a rapidly changing work environment, your team will be looking for certainty. When your team doubts your ability to deliver certainty, they may look for it elsewhere, bypassing you in the process.

As a leader, you are not paid the big bucks to navigate your team through certainty – that's the easy part. Yes, I heard you snigger as you read 'the big bucks'. But seriously, anyone can navigate certainty. A client once told me, 'The only thing I know for certain is that this s**t will still be here waiting for me on Monday morning!' You cannot guarantee certainty. Nobody can. However, the biggest mistake I see is leaders not sharing what they *do* know in uncertain situations. Your role is to make the journey through uncertainty easier for your team.

WHAT IS CERTAINTY, AND WHY IS IT SO IMPORTANT?

Certainty is the level of confidence or assurance that you – and, by extension, your team – have in something. Leadership is about determining what to do and where to go in times of uncertainty. Impactful leaders understand that establishing what is certain is an integral part of the journey. Unless you bridge the gap between vision and reality, morale, motivation, and productivity may erode. When this happens, gossip and anxiety are amplified.

Certainty shapes behaviour. Where there is certainty, there is security. Your team will feel safe in taking action. When there is a lack of certainty, your team will feel confused, fearful and hesitant. They will avoid making decisions or, at times, become impulsive in their responses. Impactful leaders help make sense of what is happening and what is about to come. Your role is to maximise certainty. Certainty is like a journey marker. When we are lost, we come back to this reference point for calibration.

THE C-WORD

Another way to think of uncertainty is that it's the by-product of change. Change – the c-word – should be considered profanity in the workplace. I cringe every time I hear a leader use the word. It is used with reckless abandon to validate poor behaviour, delays in progress and deterioration of culture. It is used as an excuse for bad leadership. 'They are so resistant to change!' cries the leader with little to no influence.

We distrust change when it is thrust upon us without context or support.

I have come to learn that we do not hate change per se; rather, we distrust change when it is thrust upon us without context or support. Let me prove my point with a simple example. What did you have for dinner last night? What did you have for dinner the night before last? What do you plan to have for dinner tonight? Your answers to all three questions are likely different, unless you are on the Soup Diet. While humans like the safety of certainty, we are bored by repetition. We naturally seek out novel experiences. Where do you think inventions come from?

Like most of my clients, I have attended the odd change masterclass in my career. They all promise a simple 500-step process that will make your change journey pain-free. I am being facetious. In theory, the steps make sense. Add people and emotions to the mix, though, and everything is up in the air. It is beneficial to have a plan, but you cannot corral staff into a change process without being met with solid resistance, unless you provide context and support.

DECLARE WHAT IS KNOWN

The often-overlooked element of achieving leadership clarity is to declare what you know. What a relief! This part isn't all that difficult – it's all about remembering to do it. What you know might be factual. It might be what you are anticipating or feeling. It might be what you *hope* will happen. As much as possible, share this with your people.

One way to declare what is known is to state that something is no longer tenable or not to be repeated. For example, 'The structure that is currently in place no longer serves our aspiration to be a customer-centric organisation,' or, 'Tony is no longer employed by this organisation.' These are certainties that help your team direct focus, energy and resources. Your role is to make certain as much as you possibly can. In most instances, declaring what is known will feel like blurting out the obvious, but don't assume everyone is aware.

I once implemented a restructure of a large team that had worked together for many years. I had been their leader for all of five minutes. While the world in which they were operating had changed drastically, business practices and roles had not. I did not know at the time what the restructure was going to look like. Rather than being like singer Miley Cyrus – 'I came in like a wrecking ball' – I wanted to identify skill sets, aspirations and passions. To prepare for the journey of change (cringe), I spoke regularly about what I knew. I was aware that our customers were no longer satisfied. I knew that the team was frustrated by cumbersome processes and systems. The organisation did not see the team as a partner – rather a painful layer of forced compliance. We needed to be customer-focused in everything that we did.

I envisaged a portfolio that added value for stakeholders and improved job satisfaction. I described the future state with great colour and movement. I needed to create both excitement and urgency. In time, my team could clearly see that the current structure was not going to help us get there. I was transparent about the fact that I had no idea how, *exactly*, we would get there. I anticipated the significant journey that lay ahead of us. We would need to reconsider current practices and challenge established rules. We had to convince senior management and our customers – both internal and external – of the benefits of any change. I committed to deliver on our aspirations.

Once I understood the team, their skills and their aspirations, I was able to structure a department that would make these aspirations a reality.

As the path became more visible, I was able to share certainties of the road ahead that, in the beginning, were unclear. I invited my team to contribute in a variety of ways that felt comfortable to them. Many were happy to share in a group meeting, and others were more comfortable providing their feedback and concerns via email. I went back to the drawing board many times because of their insight. They knew our customers better than I did.

In the final structure, some positions were made redundant. I created new roles. We welcomed new members who replaced those who sought new challenges. The constant communication of certainty amid the unknown helped us all immensely. I am not saying it was easy. Making a role redundant is always a difficult decision. It ultimately involves people and their feelings. Certainty became my journey marker in those situations. Much of this is clear to me looking back. At the time, I was running on instinct and chutzpah.

LEADING WITH CERTAINTY

You might be thinking, how do you lead your people through change and uncertainty? There are a number of key elements to consider.

Define success

First, define what success looks like. Describe the future. What will your team be doing? How will they be feeling? In my restructure example, success was a department celebrated for their commitment to customer service excellence and valuable contribution to the organisation instead of being seen as the 'corporate police'. In the beginning, I had no idea what the future structure would look like, but I was able to provide certainty about the vision of the future – this gave the team conviction about the cause.

Leaders who show a firm belief generate focus and a sense of collaboration. Your team members will be more engaged, pro-active and creative in advancing the future state. Your vision of success is your north star – your unwavering definition of purpose. It will remain a constant for both you and your team that you will depend on as your worlds change. Paint a vivid picture. Acknowledge the current situation and recognise the attempts made to address it.

Create urgency

A change initiative will be unsuccessful without a sense of urgency. A sense of urgency is the intention and momentum to progress change. A nice-to-have will never gather nor maintain momentum. In my restructure example, the urgency was the need to deliver productivity improvements and efficiency targets established for the organisation. It is much easier to control the change than to have the change control you.

Be clear about the non-negotiables

Non-negotiables are the things that will either not change or must immediately change. Be sure to explain why. Non-negotiables support the sense of urgency. Be clear about expectations. What do you expect of your team and what can everyone expect from you? How do you intend to communicate and engage with your team? Preparing a list of hypothetical, frequently asked questions will help ensure you have considered all non-negotiable matters. Keep this list to yourself, rather than circulating it – doing so will only narrow how people see your leadership, and it is not necessary.

Set dates

Be clear on dates, as much as possible. When do you *anticipate* things happening? Be sure to communicate regularly and provide updates. If you are unlikely to meet a deadline, be open and honest about it. Explain why you are unable to meet the established deadline and what the revised due date is. Do not make a habit of breaking promises. Dates should not regularly creep. It destroys trust and your credibility.

Honour meetings

Communicate often, and in different ways. You might meet with your entire team for an hour every week, or perhaps for five minutes at the start of every day. Use these meetings as an opportunity to reiterate, clarify and share information. Do not make a habit of breaking promises, and do not cancel meetings. It destroys trust and your credibility. Repetitive? Yes. Important? Absolutely!

SHARE WHAT YOU CAN

Working with teams, the most common problem I hear is that management does not communicate. After many years of leading teams, I have learnt that 'communicate', in this instance, actually means 'provide clarity'. You will find the noise dies down when your team members' concerns are clarified. Once people have enough information to buy into the change initiative, they can then begin to embrace the opportunity.

Unfortunately, under the misguided belief that it protects privacy, bad leaders skirt the facts and fill the void with confusing communication. This only fuels gossip. Leaders with poor communication skills compound this issue. This happens all too often, and even simple changes escalate into an uprising. We create our certainty.

Yes, there will always be an element of prying. Some team members feel entitled to know it all. Share what you can. Be clear about what you cannot. Engage in authentic, courageous and honest dialogue. As a (good) leader, you cannot avoid making difficult decisions, but if you are clear in your communication you will be respected.

COMMUNICATE OFTEN

The most significant determinant of success for any change program is communication. Far too often, leaders invest little to no effort in the communication strategy for their change initiative. I have counselled many who have invested considerable effort and thought into identifying the need for change, as well as the desired future state. Very few have put good thought into how they will communicate it.

Think about what you will communicate and, most importantly, how. Have a strategy to put an end to any unnecessary discussion. Never lie or make things up. Be honest. It is okay to say that you do not know, but outline how you intend to find out. Embarking on a journey with no direction is confusing. As people struggle to make sense of a new situation, they are hungry for information. At the beginning of any change initiative, seize the opportunity to share what you can, even if it is not yet the complete picture.

NEVER LIE

I am confident that, at one point in your career, you would have received an all-staff email that went a little like this:

> Good afternoon all,
>
> With mixed emotions, I announce that Tony has tendered his resignation as director to pursue other opportunities. During his time with us, Tony delivered an extensive portfolio of strategic projects, advancing the organisation's position far beyond expectation. Stakeholders regularly spoke highly of his ability to walk on water. His leadership skills were a beacon for all across the land, with his team members overwhelmed by his greatness. Join me in wishing Tony all the very best.
>
> Regards,
>
> Your Clueless CEO

Okay, so I may have gotten a little carried away with this example, but you get my point. An email like the one above is usually sent late on a Friday afternoon. Your clueless CEO hopes everyone has knocked off work early and that the email becomes lost in cyberspace, or the news is completely forgotten about over the weekend. However, everyone knows that Tony's role was no longer tenable, and an exit was negotiated.

I have personally experienced the impact of bullying from a leader. After an extensive and excruciating investigation process, my leader was moved on for failing to uphold the value of respect. The email communicating the leader's exit was not much different to my example. Everyone knew why he was moving on – we had all experienced his inability to lead. Rather than acknowledging the impact this toxic leader had on the organisation and instilling a commitment to a safe work environment, the CEO thanked the exiting leader for his brilliance. This practice only amplifies the negative experience for staff and does very little to build the kind of organisation the CEO aspires to create.

I am not saying that competent CEOs should make a habit of smearing the names of their leaders. However, there is an opportunity here to be honest, acknowledge unfortunate experiences and reinforce expected behaviours. Ideally, the all-staff email should have gone something like this:

Dear all,

As an organisation, we value respect and teamwork. We pride ourselves on being a place where people feel safe to come to work. I am committed to providing a workplace that is free from bullying and harassment.

It came to my attention that Tony conducted himself in ways that did not align with our values and expected behaviours. Tony is no longer employed with us.

The departure of any team member will impact the organisation for some time. I will communicate interim arrangements in due course.

Kind regards,

Your Impactful CEO

Although biased by my mission to eradicate toxic behaviour and leadership from organisations, the alternate email is powerful. The impactful CEO acknowledges the unfortunate situation and experiences of team members, all the while being very respectful. It leaves little room for gossip and reaffirms organisational values. When you fail to address inappropriate behaviour, you condone it.

SILENCE PERPETUATES THE FEAR

Disappointingly, during periods of uncertainty, some leaders keep a low profile. This behaviour, primarily driven by fears the leader has around engagement, sends the message that something terrible is about to happen. It is during times of uncertainty that a team needs a leader the most. As a leader, you must be the most tolerant of uncertainty. Lean on your strengths to support and navigate.

My clients always ask, 'How do I know if I have communicated enough?' There are two indicators that you are communicating effectively. Firstly, if you feel that you are over-communicating, then you are on the right track. Communicate often, using different words and different methods – paraphrase the same message for different audiences. (The underlying message should not change.) For example, if the focus is customer-centricity, use alternative ways to describe the customer experience and subsequent feedback – in meetings, via email and in individual interactions. Your communication frequency and style help all team members to hear and understand your message.

It is far better to have overcommunicated than to allow gossip and assumptions to fill the gap.

Secondly, when the questions start to die down, it is a good indicator that you are providing enough information. Initially, the questions will feel like a tsunami. Over time, the tidal wave will subside. Persist and remain steadfast and, most importantly, consistent. It can be tempting to change the approach and appease your staff as the water rises to your neck. Know that this pressure will dissipate.

Never limit your communication to the phrase 'My door is always open.' This is a throwaway statement made by someone who doesn't know what to say. What's more, only the noisy and nosy take you up on that offer. This approach strikes fear in those who are confused and concerned. Be visible, be present and engage personally. Be supportive and help your team step away from the wall. Encourage curiosity. Communicate with them regularly and check in with their concerns. Share both your hopes and concerns as you navigate together.

ALLOW THE FEELINGS

This is where most leaders struggle – dealing with the reality of human emotions. In chapter 2, you discovered the power of seeing things through others' eyes. You can never entirely prepare for – nor understand – the emotions that will unravel from a change program, but understanding your team members' values, perceptions and motivators will significantly assist.

Know that you cannot stop a reaction to change. It may be the first time your team has had any clarity, and the first time certainty has been verbalised in your team – this will trigger a reaction. Feelings are the immediate emotional response to a threat. Everyone has them, and you would have felt them yourself at the inception of the change initiative. Unlike your team, however, you have had time to come to terms with your feelings by this point. When you share your feelings, thoughts, concerns and excitement, it normalises the process for others. It also lets them know that you are not a cold-hearted narcissist.

In chapter 1, you learnt to master your emotions through self-awareness. Remain aware of your emotional state and be on the lookout for triggers. Allow for the feelings – both your own and others'. Leverage these insights you gained in chapter 2 to manage the impact that uncertainty and change can have. Remember, we all deal with challenges differently. What may seem negligible to you can seem impossible to others. Leaders who lack influence scream, 'The bus is coming – either you are on it or not.' Impactful leaders recognise the need to bring everyone along on the journey together and realise that the bus may need a few laps of the route for this to happen.

Share your thoughts and feelings. Be a voice for your team members' concerns without associating issues with a specific team member.

Vulnerability provides safety and comfort to your team. It encourages them to share.

CONCLUSION

Leading with clarity through uncertainty is daunting, no matter how many times you have done it in the past. I want you to know that you will navigate the future elegantly if you invest the time and energy to establish the foundation. Tell everyone involved what you do know. Be clear about what you do not know. Tell them how you will find the answers. Keep promises. In this chapter, you learnt about the critical need to articulate what is certain among the uncertainty of what lies ahead. After learning about the problematic skill of mastering uncertainty, you will discover how to navigate ambiguity in the next chapter.

5

Leading safely through ambiguity

Life is about not knowing, having to change, taking the moment and making the best of it, without knowing what's going to happen next.

– Gilda Radner, American actress and comedian

One of the biggest challenges for leaders today is dealing with ambiguity. Compounding this challenge is the fact that ambiguity is everywhere. I have intentionally written a chapter about ambiguity, and I want to draw attention to the distinction between ambiguity and doubt – the opposite of certainty. The *Collins English Dictionary* defines ambiguity as 'something that is unclear or confusing, or can be understood in more than one way.' On the other hand, doubt is defined as 'uncertainty about the truth, fact or existence of something.' Overcoming ambiguity requires a level of certainty.

I have come to define ambiguity as the confusion or lack of clarity in finding a way forward. It may present as a completely new situation with no familiar cues or precedents. It might be a complex situation where there are a multitude of equally attractive paths to consider. It may even be a situation that cannot be solved in the usual ways. As a leader, you will need to become comfortable with ambiguity. Few situations have a clear path to an outcome.

'Leadership is never black and white, Dale,' my mentor once told me. 'You must learn to dance in the grey.' I was an accountant at the time, in an occupation based on black and white. An accounting standard dictated every treatment. There was no grey. The concept of ambiguity was not part of the curriculum at my university – an experience shared by many.

There has never been a more relatable example of leading through ambiguity than the COVID-19 pandemic. Imagine you are the CEO of a large organisation. Overnight, you have been forced to direct every staff member to work from home until further notice. Only yesterday, from your desk, you looked out at your people buzzing in a hive of activity. Today, the office is eerily silent. You have no idea what lies around the corner. Your team members – likely lost, confused and even scared – are looking to you for clarity. *This* is why you are paid the big bucks. Who would have foreseen what was to come? No-one can predict the future – you can, however, be prepared to navigate unknown waters.

> *Leaders must become system thinkers who are comfortable with ambiguity.*
>
> – Jeffrey Immelt, former chairman and CEO of General Electric

According to research by online human resource support platform Effectory, 47 per cent of employees have little to no clarity in their role. High levels of role clarity have been proven to increase efficiency by a staggering 53 per cent, performance by 24 per cent, employee engagement by 17 per cent and employee satisfaction by 16 per cent. Global organisational consulting firm Korn Ferry found that, of 10,000 Australian respondents, 60 per cent felt they needed greater clarity in what their organisation stood for and its strategic direction. For people to continue to deliver effective outcomes during ambiguous times, they must know the purpose and values of the organisation.

Leadership is not paint-by-numbers. It can feel like driving towards a fork in the road at high speed without precise information about the right direction. Yet, when embraced, ambiguity can be very compelling. A level of ambiguity cultivates innovation. (I say 'a level' because there is a point at which ongoing ambiguity reflects incompetence.)

INTO THE UNKNOWN

If you are a parent of primary-school-age children, odds are you just sang that subheading. The sound of my daughter, Olivia, singing the soundtrack of *Frozen II* is permanently lodged in my brain. Even if you are not a parent, it is good to know that there is a soundtrack to the challenges of leadership clarity!

Dealing with ambiguity is, for the most part, something that comes with experience. It is much like having difficult conversations: there is only so much that a group of actors and a tray of muffins at a workshop can do to help you prepare for reality. We all suffer from uncertainty and doubt, especially when creating something new. I was the same when I made the transition from chief financial officer to leadership expert. There will always be an element of fear. Some leaders manage that fear well. Others visibly react.

Do not subscribe to the illusion that there is no fear. Even those who appear the most confident are managing an element of fear internally.

Impactful leaders do not need to know all the answers. They do, however, need to know the right questions to ask. As I alluded to in previous chapters, technical competency is not enough to be a leader in today's dynamic and ever-changing world. Having everyone at the executive table expedites the decision-making process and avoids unnecessarily unforeseen problems. However, too many brainstorming meetings commence with an open question along the lines of, 'So, how do we achieve [insert vague aspiration here]?' That is always the wrong question. Impactful leaders know the first question to be asked is, 'Are we all here?'

> We are at our best when the table is long, all voices are valued, and we stay curious as both teachers and learners.
>
> – Brené Brown

Your job is to leverage your team members' expertise and capability. You cannot possibly do that by telling your people what to do. Instead, you must leverage expertise and capability by asking the right questions. What are the best questions to ask, you wonder? When everyone is at the table, these questions will get results:

- Are we all here? Is anyone missing from this discussion?
- What do you think we should do in this situation?
- What do we need to stop doing that is no longer effective?
- How can I help you with that? What do you need from me for that to happen?

- Could this adversely impact another team or individual?
- Is there something we aren't seeing here?

NERVOUS LEADERS JUMP TOO SOON

Insecure leaders are nervous leaders. A nervous leader is unsure of what to do next yet determined to move forward. They are unable to sit with ambiguity. Nervous leaders focus on control. Under this influence, they almost always jump too soon. Suppress your urge to control things. Naturally, we all like to feel in control of where we are heading. When control is lost, this often results in stress as the level of ambiguity increases. As a leader, you will be at the helm of an environment that will only continue to become more complex. Let go of the notion that you need to control everything.

Like the common cold, stress and anxiety are contagious. We prefer certainty over uncertainty, regardless of how painful or unhappy our present certainty makes us. Ambiguity leads to frustration and heightened anxiety for both leaders and team members. You must manage your response to ambiguity. In chapter 1, you learnt about awareness of self. In chapter 2, you learnt about the awareness of others. Use these insights to manage how you, and your team, are likely to respond. Emotional responses are natural, as well as expected. Nervous leaders, however, are highly reactive and tend to make poorly informed decisions. Resist the urge to make a quick decision. Decisiveness is an excellent attribute of an impactful leader and requires assessing the current situation and exploring likely possibilities. Decisiveness does not mean, however, deciding in haste. This only amplifies stress across the team and compounds ambiguity.

Keep in mind that ambiguity provides you with an excellent opportunity to showcase your strong leadership. Do not waste this opportunity in your attempt to show decisiveness and steadfast problem-solving. In these instances, no-one can tell what will happen at the end of either path.

BUILD YOUR CQ TO OVERCOME THE FEAR OF AMBIGUITY

I am not fond of leadership books that are full of acronyms, but bear with me here. In my research of impactful leadership, I discovered that a new skill has emerged as a precursor to empowerment, innovation and growth. Historically, the intelligence quotient (IQ) and emotional quotient or emotional intelligence (EQ) were all the rage. Now the curiosity quotient (CQ) – the capacity for a hungry mind – is emerging as the leadership skill of the future.

Studies over the past two decades have proven that curiosity is linked to more significant learning, engagement and performance at work. Curiosity is a game-changer for leaders who are navigating ambiguity. Curiosity diffuses feelings of anxiety and overwhelm and replaces them with feelings of wonder and intrigue. According to the plethora of new studies on this emerging leadership quality, when our curiosity is triggered, we think more clearly and rationally about decisions and arrive at more creative solutions.

I love the notion of curiosity as a leadership power tool. It is more potent than IQ and EQ combined. Curiosity inspires innovation, supports your team in overcoming fear, and assists with unleashing brilliance and setting clear expectations. Even better, it is easier to develop and easily coached.

Albert Einstein said, 'Imagination is more important than knowledge.' He recognised that knowledge has limitations. Imagination, on the other hand, has no boundaries and gives rise to innovation.

So, how comfortable are you in utilising the power of curiosity to plan and innovate with your team? Impactful leaders lean on their imaginations to guide their teams through the discomfort and challenge of the unknown. Curiosity and creativity help to overcome problems and barriers in the change process. Problems, when looked at from a different angle, are opportunities in disguise. Impactful leaders know how to flip the dialogue, navigating the complexity and ambiguity that problems present. What's more, they leverage the opportunity and achieve remarkable outcomes. How can you flip your current perspective on an issue? Rather than seeing limitations, explore. Invite your team in. Many heads are better than one.

CHANGE REQUIRES CHANGE

You cannot progress a change agenda without first changing the way you do things. Without sounding cliché, if you always do what you have always done, you always get what you have always got. Sometimes it is just a tiny change. Other times, the change required may be significant. Your assumptions may need to change. Perhaps the belief system and mindset that underpin your current situation need to be reviewed. Ask yourself and your team, 'What needs to change to make change happen?' Involving many participants to share in the creative process provides both the fastest and most effective outcomes. Do not think that locking yourself away in your office with butchers' paper, sticky notes and a rainbow of highlighters is going to make a dent.

Although it makes us feel uncomfortable, the moment of ambiguity and challenge allows us to formulate a broader view of what we can do and who we can be.

Break through creativity blocks

Gather your team together and use these four proven thought starters:

1. **Scale ideas.** Include everyone and consider, at least initially, everything. Open the floor to a topic and call for all and any ideas to address it. For example, how can we reduce the time it takes to prepare our monthly report from five days to one? Or how could we encourage online self-service over in-person service delivery? Ideas will range from conservative to downright crazy. They will be built upon with greater clarity by the group.

2. **Encourage and enable collaboration.** Encourage participants to lean on their understanding and frustrations where they might not have expertise. Ask open questions such as, 'What do you think would help?', or 'How might we…?'

3. **Imagine.** It might seem like a silly idea at first, but what if…? For example, what if our team didn't produce the report? What if online self-service was the only service delivery option? What if we stopped doing it?

4. **Cut the bureaucracy.** Red tape is a sure-fire way to destroy creativity. Consider what would happen if you ignored existing processes, at least initially. It can be hard to see the possibilities when you have built boundaries. There is an element of imagination in this step, but ask the question, 'What if we didn't seek approval?'

THE INCREDIBLE POWER OF STICKY STEPS

When faced with ambiguity, accept that some of your decisions will be wrong. Although it is likely to have been the best decision at the time, it may turn out to be the wrong one. Impactful leaders are comfortable with making mistakes. Sit with that for a moment.

Great leaders embrace making decisions amidst ambiguity and then respond as new information comes to light, correcting the course of any incorrect decision.

For some leaders, the thought of making a mistake is nauseating. The good news is that you can learn to become comfortable with ambiguity. No-one expects you to relish ambiguity. There is no need to throw caution to the wind. You do, however, need to remain level headed. Consider what is likely to happen and how you will know when you are off track.

I started working with Matthew when he and his team were an entire year behind schedule. A newly appointed director, he had inherited an aspirational business plan that was both vague and poorly resourced. Matthew asked me, 'How can I possibly succeed when I have no idea where to start?' I introduced him to my favourite planning tool: Sticky Steps. My version of this leadership tool is a fusion of the process of event storming – created by author and software programming expert Alberto Brandolini – along with lean thinking and practice. Used in various forms by many facilitators, Sticky Steps develops a concrete and clear plan to achieve a goal. Starting at the end and working your way back to the beginning, it is essentially just one question – 'What needs to happen *just* before that?' Though it may look something like a sticky note crime scene, you end up with an action plan with milestones for goal oversight.

Use the handy guide below to run your own Sticky Steps process.

Activity: Using Sticky Steps to navigate change

You will need:

- One pack of green sticky notes. These will be used to articulate the goal.
- At least five packs of yellow sticky notes. These will be used to capture individual steps. You are aiming for as much detail in the process as possible.
- One pack of blue sticky notes. These will be used to capture stakeholders in the process.
- One pack of pink sticky notes. These will be used to highlight critical steps.
- Pens and markers.
- A room with a blank wall large enough for everyone to gather around and for the steps to be spread out.
- The right people in the room – an appropriate number of people who have the expertise or an understanding of the goal at hand or are divergent thinkers who will help challenge the group.

The fun begins:

1. On a green sticky note, write the overall goal. The goal must be specific. For example, the goal might be to complete the review of a program by 30 June, with the report endorsed by the board by 30 September. It might be to reduce operational costs by 20 per cent across discretionary budget lines for the next budget year. Vague goals do not have clear steps, stakeholders or milestones to monitor. Once clear, place the green sticky note at the top of your blank wall.

2. As the facilitator, ask the group, 'What needs to happen just before that?' Write that step on a yellow sticky note and place it under the goal on the far right of the wall. Each step should be small. The last step might be to send an email to all staff inviting them to the launch. 'Organise launch event' is far too broad, and sure to lead to a significant step being missed. It might be that the board endorses the report at its September meeting.

3. Now ask, 'What needs to happen just before that?'.

4. Keep working backwards. Each step is written on a yellow sticky note and added to the left of the previous step. You should be getting the gist by now.

5. When a step is a critical step, write it on a pink sticky note. A critical step is a barrier or obstacle to the next step in the process (that is, the step you just mapped out). For example, the director must provide the authorisation following the organisation's procurement policy before goods can be delivered. When reviewing your action plan, skipping this step or a deadline associated with the step will result in failure to execute. Be as specific as possible about this step.

6. When a step involves a stakeholder outside of the team involved in monitoring and delivering the goal, use the blue sticky note to identify them. Place the blue stakeholder sticky note immediately below the step. A critical step may require an external stakeholder's sign-off.

7. Keep working back until you get to the very first step.

8. Be sure to populate the reverse-engineered process with dates and identify who is accountable for each step, where appropriate.

9. Grab a coffee. Have a bite to eat. Get some fresh air. Clear your mind before you come back to review your work.

10. From left to right, make sure the steps are logical. Is a step missing? Are dates realistic? Are the right stakeholders identified? Have you provided those stakeholders with adequate time to support you? Be as detailed as possible.

11. Translate your crime scene into an action plan. You will use this to engage with your stakeholders and monitor progress. I have provided a template below to get you started but allow it to evolve. Resist the urge to complicate things. A shared spreadsheet that is updated regularly and shared at a five-minute standing meeting on a Monday morning is all you need. Interactive monitors and live information feeds are a waste of effort and money.

12. I like to use a traffic light system to monitor status:

   - **Green:** Woohoo! Milestone/step was met/delivered on time. Green signifies completion; it's not an indicator that progress is good.

   - **Amber:** Hmm… an issue is emerging. Date not yet missed, but additional oversight required.

   - **Red:** Crap! Totally missed this. Overall project in jeopardy.

   - **White/no colour:** Steady as she goes. A milestone in progress, on target or not yet due for action.

13. Ensure those involved in the project have access to the template to provide regular updates. I know it is not environmentally friendly but I suggest printing it out every Monday morning and talking about it. Make refinements as you go, incorporating updates in the template.

Sticky steps template

Project title:		Project sponsor:		Project due date:	
Step/action/ milestone	Owner	Stakeholders	Critical event (yes or no)	Due date	Status

COMMUNICATE, COMMUNICATE, COMMUNICATE

While the CEO may be the spokesperson for change, it is your role as leader to translate the organisational direction for your team. You are best positioned to communicate more frequently and more meaningfully with your people. If you only take one thing away from this chapter, it is the need to communicate. As in the previous chapter, success is determined by communication. You can never over-communicate.

Communicating what you do know is easy. Sharing what you do not know is hard. When faced with prolonged ambiguity, our imagination fills the gap. Psychologists call this amodal completion. There is a gap between what we see and what we believe; the greater this gap, the more damaging the impact. Impactful leaders are mindful of this gap and communicate often and in different ways to ensure the message is heard and absorbed. Leaders who dance around sensitive issues or avoid acknowledging their vulnerabilities and own uncertainties around what lies ahead only provide space for assumptions and gossip to run rife. Never underestimate the power and speed at which uninformed rumour spreads.

If this all seems a lot like, you are right – but I cannot stress the value of communication enough. During Melbourne's many lockdowns in 2020, my local mayor, Cr Nicole Seymour, posted almost daily on social media. While not an epidemiologist, Cr Seymour reported on local case numbers, emerging clusters and health advice. As a voice for the community, she responded to questions – calling on experts where appropriate. During what was a scary time for many, she provided comfort amidst uncertainty.

MAKE THE DECISION AT THE POINT OF CLARITY

By now, you have realised it is a rare occurrence to have absolute clarity during times of ambiguity – at least at the beginning. Impactful leaders approach change not only by defining what is absolute but by acknowledging this is the best thing to do, based on the information they currently have at hand. Gaining clarity involves navigating ambiguity. Often, leaders wait too long before they decide and commit to action. Yes, it is possible to jump too soon, as well as wait too long. Leverage your expertise, your experience, and your judgement to move forward. Waiting for certainty is not a leadership skill. You can only ever connect the dots in hindsight.

Now, armed with clarity, how do you get in there and do it? Mel Robbins, motivational speaker and author of *The 5 Second Rule: The Fastest Way To Change Your Life*, suggests that once you are armed with the information at hand, you should count down from five and then go! I love this technique. Not only is it simple, but it is also focused on the information at hand. Lean on everything you have to make a decision. Outline your path of progression and put in place checkpoints or milestones to check in as you navigate the unknown. Where needed, pivot. Incorporate new data and lean on new insights as you steer your path.

In their book *Superforecasting: The Art and Science of Prediction*, Philip Tetlock and Dan Gardner wrote, 'We are all forecasters. When we think about changing jobs, getting married, buying a home, making an investment, launching a product, or retiring, we decide based on how we expect the future to unfold.' My biggest take away from this quote is that we naturally plan for the future. We subconsciously establish certainties without knowing what the future holds.

CONCLUSION

In this chapter, you learnt about the importance of involving others and breaking things down. We also revisited the importance of communication. Leadership clarity is where most leaders stumble. In the next chapter, you will learn how impactful leaders bring it all together with the power of storytelling.

6

The power of stories

There's always room for a story that can transport people to another place.

– JK Rowling

As a leader, you are in the business of potential. Change requires the aggressive cooperation of many individuals. More than a clear vision, you require a sense of urgency. Without motivation, effort goes nowhere.

A sense of urgency provides the fuel to drive change. It supports accountability and intentional and productive activity. Without a sense of urgency, your vision is merely a good idea.

You cannot drag people along a change journey. It is unlikely that they will joyously meet you where you want them to be. Meet your team where they are at. Rather than waiting for disaster to strike and having no readiness for change, the challenge for leaders is to leverage a sense of urgency to drive action.

Impactful leaders experience a deeper level of engagement, higher levels of trust and greater momentum when they meet their people where they are at.

I have found that nothing inspires action more than a compelling story. Stories have the power to unleash potential and boost engagement. Stories provide an unfair leadership advantage.

Human beings have been telling stories for tens of thousands of years. Aboriginal Dreamtime stories are a powerful Australian example. Stories have been passed down through generations. You might be aware of how much easier it is to remember stories when they provide purpose and a clear direction. People use stories to make sense of things. Even black and white thinkers, like me, need stories. Think of stories as a framework to help people understand change and the action required for success.

STORIES ARE MEMORABLE

I recall one startling fact from when I was first learning about the art of communication: most people will have forgotten 40 per cent of what you said within 24 hours of hearing it. After a week, the amount of information forgotten increases to 90 per cent. Shared as a story, information is up to 20 times more memorable. In her *New York Times* article 'Your Brain on Fiction', author Annie Murphy Paul wrote about how MRI studies of the brain indicated little difference between the brain's activity listening to a story and encountering the same events in real life. Stories provide an emotional connection and response. Through stories, in our imagination, we can smell, feel and sense.

When you hear a story, your brain produces the chemical oxytocin. I am no neurologist, but according to Lily Brown, Director of the Center for the Treatment and Study of Anxiety at the University of Pennsylvania, oxytocin is linked to warm, fuzzy feelings. It is responsible for reduced levels of anxiety and increased levels of trust, empathy and positivity. Commonly known as the love chemical, oxytocin helps us see the world around us with rose-coloured glasses. As a result, we are more motivated to cooperate with others. While logic can convince, emotions engage and motivate. Emotions are also more memorable.

Think back to an event where you have seen a motivational speaker take to the stage to share their story. Against the odds, this amazing individual overcame unimaginable circumstances to achieve great things. You were instantly in awe, and, for just a moment, your life seemed insignificant by comparison. Their journey, challenges, successes and failures evoked deep connection, relatability and emotion. You were inspired, energised and ready to take action. So much so, you may have bought their book!

For me, learning to tell stories at work was my biggest challenge. I was scared and intimidated. I sucked at stories – well, at least, I thought I did. Some people have performed incredible feats and achieved amazing things against the odds. Their stories are inspiring. My life, up until fatherhood, was relatively dull. In the past, I relied heavily on humour and sarcasm to make my stories more interesting. Accountants did not need stories, right? Just get on with it! I naively saw our human need for stories as fluff – a performance of sorts. It took me a while to realise I needed to employ storytelling to engage my team on an emotional level. The positive impact stories have had on me in my career continues to astound me.

ALL ABOARD!

Impactful leaders know that to speed up, we must first slow down. People accept and process change at different speeds and in different ways. To enable everyone to move forward together, slow down to get everyone on the same page. This may be seen as a contradiction but it will save you time in the future. A positively engaged, supported and motivated team will achieve great things when challenged. In her book *Stories for Work: The Essential Guide to Business Storytelling*, Gabrielle Dolan writes that emotions inform your opinion on several matters, including whether you believe someone, respect them or trust them.

> *Emotions determine whether you can get behind a change agenda.*
>
> – Gabrielle Dolan

As the driver of change, you have had time to think deeply about your intended direction. You will have formulated a strategy, to some level of completion, to communicate your vision far and wide. Your team, on the other hand, have not. They will need more than a muffin and a snazzy slideshow littered with buzzwords to get on board with the idea. You need a vehicle to transport them there. Yep, you guessed it – a story!

The very thought of storytelling can be daunting. Do you share a personal story? How personal is too personal? Do you share a story of personal failure, and risk appearing incompetent? Do you share a story of success, and risk coming across as arrogant? Is humour appropriate? What are people going to think of you when all of a sudden you start to use stories? Argh! Storytelling just seems like a minefield.

By now, you have a greater understanding of your team and their needs, preferences, values and aspirations. Harness this insight and put words and imagery to your ambitions.

BEGIN WITH THE END IN MIND

A random story that rambles on (and on) – you know, those stories that end with 'you just had to be there' – does not help anyone. Stories must have a purpose. To be an impactful story-teller, first, begin with the end in mind. When planning your story, start with a clear vision of your desired destination. Educator, author, businessman and keynote speaker Stephen R Covey, in his book *The 7 Habits of Highly Effective People: Powerful Lessons in Personal Change*, writes that all things are created twice. The first, he suggests, is a mental creation. The second is a physical creation. Covey likens the process of creation to the construction of a house. It is first created in detail as a set of architectural plans before you hammer the first nail in place. Stories are similar. You may not have a detailed blueprint, but you must, at the very least, have a plan that outlines the journey to your aspiration. Stories for change require thought.

A few years ago I had joined an organisation as their finance manager, leading the finance department. The team had been through a challenging period with their previous leader. Someone they trusted had lied to them over many years. To make matters worse, the organisation provided the team with little support to heal. I had a mandate to rebuild the team. Despite my efforts, the team was stuck and resisted all invitations to move into the future. I expressed my frustration to my mentor at the time. She suggested I use storytelling as a tool for change. I cringed. I sighed. More than likely, I rolled my eyes.

Why would my mentor suggest I tell fairytales? You see, I did not know what storytelling was. I had no idea how powerful it could be. My mentor said to me that stories could help leaders meet their people where they are at. She introduced me to the simple formula for powerful storytelling – the Pixar Pitch.

ONCE UPON A TIME…

Pixar Animation Studios is one of the most successful studios in movie-making history. *Toy Story*, released in 1995, grossed US$374 million worldwide at the box office. Worldwide box office sales from the *Toy Story* franchise of three films have surpassed US$3 billion.

With more than 20 feature films under its belt, Pixar knows a thing or two about telling a story. Former Pixar storyboard artist Emma Coats cracked the code for powerful storytelling. Coats, harnessing her insights from her time at Pixar, composed a series of 22 tweets outlining story basics. In the fourth tweet Coats highlighted that almost every Pixar film shares the same narrative DNA. This is the framework my mentor shared with me. This deep structure of storytelling, involving just six sequential sentences, is known as the Pixar Pitch. It goes like this:

1. Once upon a time, there was…

2. Every day…

3. One day…

4. Because of that…

5. Because of that…

6. Until finally…

To prove how powerful the simple formula is, Coats used the Pixar Pitch when pitching the plot to *Finding Nemo*:

1. Once upon a time, there was a widowed fish, named Marlin, who was extremely protective of his only son, Nemo.

2. Every day, Marlin warned Nemo of the ocean's dangers and implored him not to swim far away.

3. One day, in an act of defiance, Nemo ignores his father's warnings and swims into the open water.

4. Because of that, he is captured by a diver and ends up in the fish tank of a dentist in Sydney, Australia.

5. Because of that, Marlin sets off on a journey to recover Nemo, enlisting the help of other sea creatures along the way.

6. Until finally, Marlin and Nemo find each other, reunite and learn that love depends on trust.

It blew my mind! An entire feature-length film was based on six simple sentences.

THE GATEWAY TO POSSIBILITY

My first experience with storytelling felt like a nightmare. With the end in mind, my goal was to acknowledge my team's journey and concerns. I needed to slow down to enable everyone to catch up. I had not abandoned my vision for the future, but I needed to let my team know that we were in this together. I needed to create a baseline – a line in the sand, you could say. I spent an entire week preparing for a story that would take no more than one minute to deliver. I decided our next planning day was the perfect opportunity to share the story.

I remember the nervousness I felt as my team dragged themselves into the conference room. Usually high energy, I felt nauseous. I was not my usual self. My team could sense something was different. They asked me if I was okay. I had no idea how my story was going to be received. I had told my mentor that I felt it would seem odd or out of character to spring a story. She suggested starting with a jolt to the mind. I needed to shift their mind away from where we were. As everyone took their seats, I slowly made my way to the front of the room. Without formality, I asked them to close their eyes. To be honest, I needed them to not be looking at me! I told them to imagine that I was sitting at the end of their bed, about to tell them a story. When I am in bed, I feel comfortable, safe and secure. Sure, the creep factor of this image was through the roof, but instantly I could sense the energy in the room had changed. I began to tell my story, which went a little something like this:

Once upon a time, there was a finance team.

Every day, this team of experts came to work wanting to make a difference.

One day, they learnt that the leader they had trusted had lied to them.

Because of that, rumours were flying around the organisation about what had happened. The team blamed themselves for what he had done.

Because of that, they lost enjoyment in their work, undermining the teamwork they were known for.

Until finally, a new leader with a strong vision for the future came to support them to move forward and achieve amazing things.

I took a long slow breath. Nausea subsided. I told them to open their eyes. I waited for the looks of confusion and the eye rolls. The groans and the giggles. The most resistant member broke the silence of the team. I was prepared for the interrogation. 'Thank you,' he said. No-one had previously acknowledged their journey or their feelings. We did laugh (a lot) about the creepiness of imagining me sitting at the end of their bed, but they understood my approach. We achieved so much in that session, and the team began to find their groove again.

Your story

Now it's your turn to write your story. Below, I have expanded on each of the six sequential sentences to get you on your way.

1. **Once upon a time, there was...** Set the context for your story. For example, who are you talking about? Where are you? What year is it?

2. **Every day...** Describe the rituals and habits of your character(s). What happened over and over again?

3. **One day...** This is the catalyst for change. Leverage the sense of urgency. What is the catalyst? Be specific yet as brief as possible. You do not want to bore your audience.

4. **Because of that...** Describe an outcome as a result of the catalyst. What immediately happened as a result? It may be positive or negative.

5. **Because of that...** Ideally, this would be a positive outcome of progressive change. However, if your story is one of acknowledgement of the present state, it may be another acknowledgement of a pain point.

6. **Until finally...** Describe the future state. It may involve recognition of where your audience is today – the beginning of possibility.

STORIES HAVE IMPACT

As soon I became more comfortable telling stories, I started using them regularly. I found that stories helped improve the impact of my message. My client, Jackie, experienced this too. For many years Jackie had used devastating statistics to convey the importance of her programs that she ran in primary schools. Over time, however, the statistics she was sharing about the deterioration in levels of literacy lost their impact. I worked with Jackie to convey the same message, but with a story. Rather than picking up the clicker to commence her presentation at a budget meeting, Jackie told the board of directors a story:

> When Frank was four years old, he dreamed of being a doctor when he grew up. He would head for the dress-up box at kindergarten and don the white coat and stethoscope, operating on dolls and teddy bears who were 'injured'.
>
> One day, Frank took a numeracy and literacy test. The results put him significantly behind the national average for his age. Frank was falling behind his classmates and soon lost confidence. He became more disengaged.
>
> Fortunately, Frank's teacher identified his different learning style and found resources to help. Today, Frank is getting excellent grades in high school and is well on his way to fulfilling his dream of becoming a doctor.

Jackie's storytelling resulted in the doubling of her program's funding. The board of directors could imagine, relate to and connect with the story of Frank. Logic can convince, but emotions engage and motivate. Jackie was comfortable with telling stories, but she hadn't considered the power storytelling could have in a formal setting. Her experience is an example of how you can adapt the structure of the Pixar Pitch.

I was not personally a fan of starting my story with the phrase 'once upon a time'. It felt too much like a fairytale. I did, however, need a foolproof structure to follow to the letter for my first story. As your storytelling matures, you can adapt the script. You might start with, 'It was five years ago today…' or 'When two teams merged 12 months ago…' or even 'When I accepted the role of manager, I had the dream of…'. As you can see from Jackie's story example, the framework can be adapted to support your purpose. I must admit I do find it funny when I work with teams and everyone gets up to speak with the opening line, 'Once upon a time.' Despite this, I continue to teach the six-sentence structure to all of my clients to establish a foundation for storytelling.

BRIDGING CERTAINTY, AMBIGUITY AND THE FUTURE

Impactful storytellers understand the point of their story. They also use real stories – they do not make them up. While they may not recite their story word for word perfectly every time, they retell the narrative with conviction. Consider:

· What is the purpose of your story?

· What is it about?

· What happened, and to whom?

· How does your story relate to your audience, their reality and your vision for the future?

After all, you don't really understand it unless you can explain it to a six-year-old.

– Albert Einstein

If you are confused, your audience will be baffled. Be sure to know, from memory, the key elements and characters of your story.

Twelve tips for effective storytelling

1. **Relax**. No-one knows how your story was meant to go.

2. **Don't say that!** People may never look at you the same way if you share too much information. Avoid getting too personal.

3. **It's not about you**. If you feel your story is self-indulgent, it most likely is.

4. **Know your audience.** What are their preferences for receiving and processing information? What language do they use?

5. **Do not bore.** Keep your story concise yet powerful. Avoid the use of numbers and data unless they are essential to the story.

6. **Why now?** Explain the urgency for change. Why can't we just keep doing what we are doing?

7. **Describe the promised land**. What will we be doing and feeling in a different and better future compared to what we are doing and feeling today?

8. **How will you get there?** Explain the journey. You are not psychic, but outline the journey based on what you already know.

9. **Acknowledge obstacles**. Identify any challenges you anticipate along the way – even if they're minor – and explain how you will overcome them. Pre-empting possible setbacks or delays avoids the disappointment and potential loss of momentum and motivation when they arise.

10. **Engage.** Be open to questions, and answer them honestly.

11. **Practise**. When you are using a story as a tool for change, it is helpful if you do not fumble. Practise in front of a mirror. If it helps, rehearse the story in front of a few people and gauge their reaction.

12. Collect stories. Once you realise how powerful stories are, you will start adding them to your library. Impactful leaders have lots of stories and know when and how to use them.

CONCLUSION

This brings us to the end of part II. You have learnt all about leadership clarity. Providing clarity is the most significant task for leaders, yet it trips many up. Your job is sense-making for your teams. To support understanding and engagement, first, declare what is certain. Acknowledge, discuss, interpret and navigate ambiguity. While difficult, it is not impossible. The gap between where you and your team are and where you aspire to be is bridged with stories.

In part III, you will learn about leadership energy. Leadership sucks at times. I have found myself thinking that it would be so much easier if people were not involved! Keeping at it when the challenges seem all too great requires fuel. In the final section of this book, I will show you how to find that fuel and build huge reserves of it, to carry yourself through the tough times.

LEADERSHIP ENERGY

7

Pioneering leadership

Fear is a reaction. Courage is a decision.

– Sir Winston Churchill

Leaders can be pioneers. History is full of people whose courage changed the world. Rosa Parks, the African American civil rights advocate, went to jail for refusing to give up her seat on a bus to a white man, sparking the American civil rights movement. Dr Martin Luther King Jr, social rights activist and leader of the American civil rights movement, famously declared, 'I have a dream.' Former US President John F Kennedy had a vision of landing a man on the moon. At 17, Malala Yousafzai, a female education advocate, became the youngest person to win the Nobel Peace Prize. Greta Thunberg, an environmental activist, won an essay competition at the age of 15, publicly challenging world leaders to take immediate action against climate change. These are but a few of the courageous individuals who have made an impact on the world. Brave leaders make remarkable contributions. Leaning on their personal *why* they have led and continue to show greatness. Greatness takes courage. A movement requires courage.

Courage does not imply the absence of fear – courage is taking action in spite of fear. It is what empowers you to act despite the absence of certainty.

Courage is not an intellectual quality or a skill that can be taught. Much like wisdom, courage comes from experience. You can only build courage through repeated experiences of personal risk-taking. Courageous leaders are those who can push through uncomfortable situations and make difficult decisions. They do not back down when things get too hard. Courage distinguishes impactful leaders from mediocre leaders. Courageous leaders are respected.

COURAGE TRUMPS CONFIDENCE

Many people confuse confidence with courage. When working with clients, I regularly hear, 'I just don't have the confidence.' What they mean is that they do not have enough courage to tackle the problem at hand. The *Macquarie Dictionary* defines confidence as 'full trust; belief in the trustworthiness or reliability of a person or thing; assurance.' Courage is defined as 'the quality of mind that enables one to encounter difficulties and danger with firmness or without fear; bravery.' Confidence is a measure of certainty. Courage, on the other hand, is a mindset. Courage is a prerequisite of confidence, which comes from learning. To learn, try new things. Trying new things takes courage.

I was fortunate enough to have been in the audience when bestselling author Brené Brown came to Melbourne in 2019.

'The future of leadership belongs to the brave', she told the audience at the packed Melbourne Exhibition and Convention Centre. 'The thing we are missing more than anything right now is courage in leadership.' Cheers and applause filled the auditorium.

From personal experience, I know that an entire organisation benefits from courageous leadership. Courageous leaders implement change faster and with better-than-anticipated outcomes. Courage allows staff at all levels of the organisation to push perceived boundaries and take on larger and more complex projects. Courageous teams deal better with change and are collectively more assertive about matters that are important to them. Courage is contagious. A fearless leader empowers their team to try, trust and share more.

Courage allows you to take the first step. You might fail. You might get it wrong. You might, on the other hand, achieve something incredible! Courage helps you test the limits of your potential. Courage also allows you to relinquish control. When you empower and delegate to others, you bestow a level of control. When you delegate, you are showing trust. Trust requires courage. This, in turn, creates more trust. Courageous leaders form resilient and deep relationships through this process.

Courage allows you to vocalise – to speak up and share your truth. This includes owning your mistakes. Courage breeds vulnerability. If you struggle with vulnerability and shame, place your focus on being brave.

COURAGE MAKES CHANGE POSSIBLE

Courageous leaders seek and leverage opportunities. The status quo is the path of least resistance. It is the easiest path, but it does not result in innovation and growth. Change is impossible without courage.

Fear and comfort are bad for business.

One of my favourite examples of courageous leadership is the story of Alan Mulally, former president and CEO of Ford Motor Company. When Mulally joined Ford in 2006, it was a car manufacturer that, year after year, operated at eye-watering losses. In 2006, Ford achieved the forecast operating loss of a staggering US$17 billion! Mulally spoke of financial management reports littered with green traffic lights indicating that budgetary losses were on track. It took courage to talk about what many others were no doubt thinking: celebrating the deterioration of a large organisation made absolutely no sense. Waking up to the reality of an unsustainable business model, Ford borrowed more than US$20 billion to finance major equipment and overhaul processes. In a show of courage, Ford secured the borrowings against its brand assets. To further boost profits and reduce the bleeding of cash, Mulally sold the company's investment in brands including Aston Martin, Land Rover, Jaguar, Volvo and Mazda. Mulally's courageous move paid off. As the global financial crisis struck and US car sales plummeted, Ford regained market share. Unlike its Detroit competitors including General Motors and Chrysler, Ford avoided bankruptcy and did not require emergency loans from the US government. Courageous and informed decisions returned Ford to profitability. No doubt Mulally faced ridicule on his journey of organisational transformation and recovery. As a fearless leader, he held firm to his convictions and is widely credited as the man who saved Ford.

Indra Nooyi, former CEO of PepsiCo, is another courageous leader. In 2006, Nooyi anticipated changing consumer preferences for healthier foods and beverages – particularly amongst millennials. Nooyi introduced PepsiCo's strategy to complement the company's core soft drink and snack business with healthy foods and beverages such as diet drinks and lower-calorie snacks. Coca-Cola, at the time, ignored the emerging trends, concentrating more on sugar-based soft drinks. According to global media company Forbes, between 2011 and 2017, PepsiCo shares surged 70 per cent, compared with only 15 per cent for Coca-Cola. Coca-Cola has since introduced more low and no-sugar varieties.

Courageous leaders inspire others when they take action.

There are many examples of leaders who have made courageous decisions to build and grow great global brands, such as Amazon's Jeff Bezos, Alibaba's Jack Ma and Tesla's Elon Musk. It is only by ignoring conventional wisdom, breaking a few rules, pushing rigid boundaries and daring to be adventurous that something remarkable is born.

Organisations devoid of courageous leadership lack innovation, customer growth and employee retention and attraction. Recent history provides countless examples of organisations that failed to be courageous. Research by Capgemini Consulting, a global strategy and transformation firm, indicates that since the year 2000, 52 per cent of Fortune 500 companies have ceased to exist. These were large multinational companies that have gone bankrupt, were acquired or fell victim to digital disruption. This level of cannibalisation will only rise with the exponential growth in technological advancement. Kodak is a case in point. The graphic and imaging technology company dominated the photography and photographic film and print industry for more than 100 years. Despite developing (see what I did there?) digital photography technology and the first digital camera, it never made it to market. Kodak had become comfortable being the industry leader and did not see the need to be courageous. It was not brave enough to consider a future where a consumer did not need film or printed photographs. Kodak saw digital photography as the enemy rather than an opportunity.

As an impactful leader, what do you foresee the future of your sector, industry or profession to be? When we are brave to imagine, it spurs a sense of urgency. Aspiring accountants often ask me about the future of accounting. I do not see rows of brown suits playing with calculators. Artificial intelligence software will replace a significant component of the work accountants currently do in a fraction of the time and cost. Artificial intelligence software is already able to analyse complex data and anticipate emerging trends, threats and opportunities, helping management to make strategic decisions using accurate up-to-the-second data. The future of accountancy will be more people focused.

Be brave enough to anticipate a future where your skills may no longer be relevant. If you are not courageous enough to drive change, change will drive you.

If you are not courageous enough to drive change, change will drive you.

NAME YOUR FEARS

I do not intend to trivialise fear or anxiety; I understand how debilitating anxiety can be and by no means intend to dilute the realities of mental illness. However, it's helpful to remember that fear, after all, is just a chemical. Fear is a chain reaction in the brain triggered by a stress stimulus. That trigger might be your manager putting you on the spot in a meeting, or asking you to make a presentation to a large audience. Maybe you have to make a difficult decision that could negatively impact others. Your heart starts to race and your breathing quickens. You might find yourself in the middle of a flight-or-fight response. You sense something is dangerous and that you should be afraid. Fear, at that moment, feels very real.

Let me first make it clear that fear does serve a protective function. Fear provides a critical survival-related function in the face of a threat by activating a range of defensive behaviours. As a natural biological response to your surroundings, this type of fear cannot be eliminated. This is different from the fear that most often gets in leaders' way: the feeling of hesitation and doubt without the presence of a threat to your safety. I describe this fear as:

- **F**alse
- **E**vidence
- **A**ppearing
- **R**eal.

Many leaders become so paralysed by fear that they actively avoid people and situations. Some freeze in the moment. Fear does not help a leader's credibility.

So how do you move past fear? I have learnt that naming my fears helps to reduce the physical impact they have on me. I am not saying I am fearless, but I am more in control of my reactions. When you name your fears, it takes away some of the power they have over you. Telling your spouse, partner or friend what you are most afraid of is one way to cut fear off at the knees. If you are not comfortable with speaking about your fears, write them down. When you acknowledge your fears, you start the process of finding solutions to them.

Failing to recognise and name your fears only allows your brain to make wild projections about the future. Never under-estimate the catastrophic power of your imagination. Otherwise known as your reticular activating system, it is the part of the brain that filters your world through the parameters that you give it. For example, if you take the stage to give a speech and tell yourself, 'Don't stuff this up!', you most likely will.

Activity: Name that fear!

Grab your journal, a pen and, of course, a hot cup of coffee. Find yourself a comfortable chair or a nice quiet corner. Think about the things you would do if you had no fear. I am particularly interested in your leadership fears – the things that hold you back from being a courageous leader. Perhaps it is speaking up and sharing your opinion in meetings. Maybe you fear having a frank discussion with an overbearing colleague. Be specific:

· What is your fear?
· What is the situation?
· What is the *actual* fear?
· For each fear, list what could go wrong. Let your imagination run wild. It is easy to fall into the trap of negative thinking.

With your new list of catastrophes, turn your focus now to possibilities. List everything that could go right. What would happen if you took that first step, everything went to plan and it did not turn out to be the train wreck you had vividly anticipated? What then sits between you and an incredible outcome? The goal is not to eliminate the fear; however, do not be surprised if this happens to be a silver lining. The goal is to put structure, support and a backup plan in place to tackle the fear, should it emerge.

THE CIRCUS IS COMING TO TOWN

Too often, we wait. We wait to get the complete picture, we wait for all of the facts, and sometimes we wait for approval. Then, and only then, do we decide that it is time to get to work and take action. The circus does not wait. The circus shows up. As a kid, I always felt great surprise to see trailers parked on a field for what would soon be a circus tent of wonder. The circus shows up and sells tickets. Its members perform. They pack it all up and move on to the next town. The circus is an excellent example of courage.

Courageous leaders do not shirk bold action because they fear failure. They do not seek adulation or wane in the face of criticism. Courageous leaders know how to navigate negative and loud voices. They lean on their *why* for guidance when pressure mounts.

> *Courage is the ability to show up when you can't be sure of the outcome.*
>
> – Brené Brown

In chapter 5, I introduced you to Mel Robbins, motivational speaker and author of *The 5 Second Rule – The Fastest Way To Change Your Life*, and her tool for taking action. Once armed with the information at hand, Robbins suggests counting down from five and then go! I have used this technique many times, and it is impressive how much courage you can muster in five seconds. Try it. It may just be the nudge that you needed. But, just like the circus, make calculated decisions. Lion tamers invest years in learning their craft. What appears to be certain death to the audience is a series of calculated decisions backed by years of practice with that lion, resulting in a dramatised performance.

At its extreme, courage can cross the line of foolhardiness. While profoundly idiotic, it does take courage to jump off a cliff and assemble the plane on the way down. Gather evidence and seek advice. Always make an informed decision. You may never recover from a foolish decision.

Seven tips for building courage

1. **Get comfortable with being uncomfortable.** Courage requires you to take a personal risk. The process will feel uncomfortable. You will feel vulnerable. Lean on your self-awareness insights from chapter 1 as you navigate.

2. **Seek feedback.** Leadership is a lifelong journey. So is courage. Invite feedback. Listen deeply. Implement feedback that will help you grow as an impactful leader. Refer to 'Ten steps to powerful feedback' in chapter 1.

3. **Ditch the rose-coloured glasses**. Take a step back and see the situation for what it is. Courageous leaders confront reality. You are not the only person to see it – you need to be the one who takes action in light of it.

4. **Engage in genuine conversations.** 'I don't think this is the right approach', 'We need to be more specific', 'I sense we are off the mark' and 'This is not what I value' are great openers to difficult conversations. Courageous leaders speak up. They do not skirt the sensitive issue – they embrace authentic dialogue that may be uncomfortable, confronting and cause conflict. Not everyone will be happy to hear what you have to say. Communicate openly, honestly and often. Revisit part II of this book to refresh your approach to communication.

5. **Diversify**. Surround yourself with different opinions, experiences and values. Read widely. Ask questions of others who don't share your opinion. Gain insights from people with experiences that contrast with yours. You may find it uncomfortable. You might

even feel annoyed by the people who differ in their opinion. You do not need to validate your opinion nor nullify theirs. This exposure can help you to make an informed decision before you jump into action.

6. **Be decisive.** The only thing worse than a leader who makes reckless decisions is one that makes no decisions. Indecisive leaders are not respected.

7. **Take action.** Consultation is a great engagement tool, but I have seen it bring progress to a grinding halt. It is like being on a rocking horse: there is lots of momentum, but no-one is going anywhere. Once you have finished with the consultation process, make a decision. Count down from five. Monitor for deviation and take corrective action where required. Be open to fine-tuning. There are many individuals and teams who are great at planning but stink at taking action.

CONCLUSION

In this chapter, you learnt that courageous leaders step out, knowing there is a possibility of failure. Followers do not expect leaders to be perfect. They do, however, need to embrace strength and courage in times of uncertainty. It takes guts to stand out. It takes conviction to endure ridicule. Not all leaders can tolerate this for lengths of time. Impactful leaders possess a trait that endures these challenges: it is called grit. You will learn about grit in the next chapter.

8

Get gritty!

It is hard to fail but it is worse never to have tried to succeed.

– Theodore Roosevelt

As in life, leadership will throw things at you. You will face countless challenges. You will make decisions that turn out to be incorrect. You will draw criticism. You can bury your head in the sand and hope the storm passes, or you can get on and find a solution. These roadblocks will require a unique attribute to overcome. Success in these situations has very little to do with talent, IQ or EQ, and more to do with what I call grit. Grit is where passion and perseverance intersect. Impactful leaders have grit. In this chapter, I will clarify the difference between courage and grit.

Dr Angela Duckworth, a psychology professor and author of *Grit: The Power of Passion and Perseverance*, spent many years researching the determinants of successful people. Duckworth has proven that grit is a greater predictor of success than intelligence. She says: 'Grit is having a goal you care about so much that it organizes and gives meaning to almost everything you do. Grit is holding steadfast to that goal over time. Even when you fall down. Even when you screw up. Even when progress toward that goal is halting or slow.'

Research involving 790 United Kingdom university students and graduates across three studies found that successful students had higher levels of grit. Published by the University of Bolton, the research reported that grittier students were more likely to demonstrate an increased level of self-control, mental wellbeing, life satisfaction, feelings of worth, resilience and a growth mindset. Gritty students were more likely to have lower levels of perceived stress. These gritty, high-achieving students were also more likely to overcome personal challenges and obstacles and persevere despite facing barriers. They were able to identify their long-term goals and strive towards their achievement. Excellent time management and prioritisation skills were evident in successful students, along with their ability to express self-awareness. These students held a positive attitude towards learning and life in general and stressed the importance of feedback and constructive criticism in their personal development and growth.

Ant Middleton, former British soldier, adventurer, television presenter and author of *The Fear Bubble: Harness Fear and Live Without Limits*, says that 90 per cent of Special Air Service (SAS) candidates fail the qualifying test. 'The majority of people don't have what it takes,' Middleton says. 'Of the 202 people in my course, just eight of us passed.' Despite a distinguished military career and athletic builds, it is grit that allows them to endure the harsh test conditions. Candidates who fail can return and attempt the qualifying test again. The SAS does not report on the success rate of candidates who repeat the qualifying test. I wonder how many develop the grit to succeed.

LEADERSHIP SUCKS

Have you ever felt the need to bash your head against a wall repeatedly? Yup, leadership can suck! Things would be so much easier if other people did not get involved. Not only can the tasks of leading others feel torturous, but it can also feel very lonely. Confidants start to thin out naturally as you work your way up the ladder in your organisation and career. Many of the leaders who decide to work with me do so just before they are about to throw in the towel.

In many instances, you are the only one pushing a change agenda. Sustaining these challenges builds impact and influence.

When I discovered the power of grit and focused on developing it as a leader, I experienced the following benefits:

·   **I found increased courage.** As an ambivert (yes, that's a thing – someone who has a balance of extrovert and introvert features in his personality), I harboured some fears about the outcome of my chosen direction. Grit gave me the determination to keep going. As Dory, the regal blue tang amnesiac from Pixar's *Finding Nemo*, would say, 'Just keep swimming.'

·   **I had improved focus.** Grit made me even more determined to bring to life my vision of a customer service focused department with staff empowered to make tangible improvements. Despite resistance and setbacks, I remained steadfastly committed to the future state. This focus allowed me to evaluate alternatives and find dynamic solutions when faced with a roadblock.

· **I learnt to reframe.** Grit helped me to reframe my approach to problems and see things from a different perspective. Perseverance helps you to sit back and take a look from a different angle.

Just like every 10-step recovery program, one important component of grit that I am currently working on is the ability to acknowledge that I can't control everything.

As a leader, grit helps remind you why you do what you do. As you become grittier, you deepen your personal *why*.

YOUR INNER DRILL SERGEANT

Put simply, grit is a measure of your commitment to a cause. In his book *Outliers: The Story of Success*, journalist Malcolm Gladwell popularised the notion that it takes 10,000 hours of devotion to a craft or skill for mastery. Drawing on a study by Anders Ericsson, a researcher in the psychological nature of expertise and human performance, Gladwell's message is that people are not born geniuses. He asserts that people get to a level of success through effort and effort alone, which is just another term for grit.

Do you have a passion for something so great that you spend countless hours doing it? You may wake before the sun or soldier on well into the night. It may be the refinement of a skill, a sport or a hobby. Discomfort is irrelevant when you have a laser-like focus. It's like the Olympic hopeful, waking at 4 am and training for four hours, six days a week.

Unfortunately, grit does not permeate all aspects of your life. There will always be tasks and activities that fail to bring you joy and engagement. You spend the minimum amount of time on these just to ensure that they get done. Leadership is the same.

There will be elements of leadership and your role as a pioneer that you greatly enjoy. When highly engaged, you invest your time and energy to see it through. There will also be elements that get very little, even none, of your attention. Despite their importance to your team, you find it hard to build the momentum to tackle these. In many instances, they go unaddressed. Perhaps the Olympic hopeful never getting their uniform in the wash before training is a great example of the limits of their passion?

There are two common reasons for giving certain tasks less attention than others: either you fail to understand the needs of others, or you lack courage. When you can't understand the needs of others, it's difficult to see that the task or activity is essential or beneficial to your team. You fail to see the importance because it is not crucial to you. The lens through which you see the world creates bias. When you lack courage, you are fearful and may avoid the task or activity altogether.

I once worked for a director who despised engagement. He could think of nothing more wasteful of his time than to engage with his senior leaders. Craig, for the sake of the story, would cancel team meetings minutes before their scheduled start. As time progressed, the time between the email advising of the cancellation and the anticipated commencement came down to the wire. It was almost a sport. Craig would rather gouge his eyes out with a fork than engage with others. He was not a people person. He was a dictator. The team began to ignore meeting invitations, and soon the concept of open communication and engagement ceased to exist. Craig lacked courage. Craig was not an impactful leader.

But how do you push through and grow grit when you feel that the task or activity is a waste of your time, or you lack courage? Think about the end game. Rather than thinking about what could go wrong, think about what could go right. Draw on the tips that I shared in the activity 'Name that fear!', which you will find in chapter 7. What if everything went right? If you were to endure, what awaits you on the other side? It must, of course, be something that brings you closer to your desired future state.

Success as a leader doesn't happen overnight. It is a hard slog, requiring passion, determination and consistency. It requires grit. Leadership and grit are lifelong journeys. You need to have an inner drill sergeant to kindly but firmly keep you on track. English playwright John Heywood is quoted as saying, 'Rome wasn't built in a day, but they were laying bricks every hour.' I have been to Rome. The city's stone-paved roads are extensive. It took grit to complete a task akin to draining the ocean with a cup.

HANG IN THERE

Impactful leaders, just like high achievers, have perseverance. Even when they are already at the top of their game, they always strive for improvement. Through sacrifice and pain, their commitment remains steadfast. Impactful leaders hang in there. Hanging in there requires grit. In the words of philosopher and country music legend Dolly Parton, 'If you want the rainbow, you gotta put up with the rain.'

In the late 1960s, Walter Mischel, then a professor of psychology at Stanford University, developed an ingenious experiment to test the willpower of children. One at a time, a group of four-year-olds were brought into a small room and sat at a table in front of a marshmallow. Next to the marshmallow was a bell. Each child was told that the observer would leave the room and that only when she returned could the child eat the marshmallow. They were told that if they rang the bell, the observer would return, and they could eat the marshmallow. However, if they were patient and waited for the observer to return without ringing the bell, they could have two marshmallows. You may know of this research – it became known as the Marshmallow Test. Mischel was interested in the study of temptation and delayed gratification. In the early 1980s, Mischel resumed the experiment with the same group of children, who were now much older. In particular, Mischel was intrigued by the correlation between the child's ability to delay gratification and their academic outcomes. Revisiting as many of the study's original participants as possible, Mischel found a direct correlation between the ability to wait and academic results. Children who had been able to wait at least 15 minutes before eating a marshmallow had SAT (a standardised test widely used for college admissions in the United States) scores that were 210 points higher than those children who rang the bell within the first 30 seconds.

Recall a time where you persevered with something. What was the challenge and what was the outcome? Can you recall what that achievement felt like? Help your team identify a time when they have shown grit. Ask your team to think of a challenging experience they got through. This is the proof they can persevere, and it lays the foundation for them to build upon in the future.

GRIT DRIVES PERFORMANCE

The most significant benefit of grit is that it drives individual and team performance. More than organisational culture, organisational grit is where leaders need to focus their energy. Sure, culture has more appeal, but culture reflects the people at the end of the day – not the other way around. Gritty organisations are unstoppable. Grit is synonymous with resilience. Individuals and teams that are gritty are more effective and can weather all sorts of storms.

Disbanded in 2012, Chumbawamba was an English rock band that drew on genres such as punk rock, pop and fold. The band is best known for its 1997 hit song *Tubthumping* with the lyrics, 'I get knocked down, but I get up again' – the anthem of leadership grit. Let it be your anthem for impactful leadership.

Seven steps to build grit

1. **Actively seek feedback.** Effective feedback is specific. Ask a colleague or trusted friend, 'What did I do well?' Also ask, 'What is something I should keep in mind for next time?' Refer to 'Ten steps to powerful feedback' in chapter 1.

2. **Aim to do one small thing better than you did it before.** It may be incorporating some of the feedback you solicited. It may be reviewing, but not overthinking, your performance. What marginal improvement could you make that, over time, transforms your capability?

3. **Do not give up!** I get it, it can be so easy to quit. You gave it all you could, right? Keep at it. Remember your *why*. Channel your inner drill sergeant.

4. **Encourage others.** Encourage others to remember why they started. Channel your inner aerobics instructor. Come on! You've got this! (Bonus points if you wear a sweatband.)

5. **Celebrate small victories.** I know some of you sighed when you read that. I am not asking you to keep a gratitude journal, but do celebrate the wins, however small. They all add up. Impactful leaders high-five themselves and their teams.

6. **Look to the future.** If everything goes to plan, what will it look like on the other side? Share that with others. It helps them engage with your vision faster.

7. **Keep at it.** Hang in there.

A WORD OF CAUTION

Grit is powerful, and a great leadership strength to possess. Like all leadership strengths, when amplified they can lead to unintended consequences. A gritty person can be overbearing. Like an aerobics instructor or a host on the reality TV show *The Biggest Loser*, enthusiasm and passion can grate and wear others down. Be mindful of how you may impact others.

CONCLUSION

In this chapter, you learnt about the power of grit. It may be the first time you have heard of it. Giving it a label helps you to understand this intangible determinant of success. I have come to realise that impactful leaders are ordinary managers with an extraordinary amount of grit. In the next and final chapter, you will learn about mindset. Mindset underpins leadership energy. It controls your ability to be courageous and gritty.

9

Lead at your best

Whatever the mind can conceive and believe, it can achieve.

– Napoleon Hill, author of *Think and Grow Rich*

I am not the type to wake up at 5 am, guzzle down a green all-natural raw foods smoothie, meditate for 30 minutes before going for a run, then capture my innermost thoughts in a hemp-covered journal. I am *not* a morning person. I am a night owl and do my best work in the calm of the evening – free from distractions and interruptions. My mind is most active and effective later in the day.

We each have different optimal performance rhythms. We also focus on being mindful in very different ways. By all means, if you are a morning person who starts the day with your rear end directed to the sky in a tranquil downward-dog yoga pose, keep at it! If you like to recover with adult colouring books, colour away! There is no judgement here.

Mindfulness is when you focus on being intensely aware of what you are seeing and feeling in the moment, without judgement. But this chapter is not about mindfulness. This chapter is about mindset. So, let's put the chimes back in the box. *Ding!*

Impactful leaders know they must be at their best to lead both themselves and others. Without the right mindset, leading others into the unknown and meeting challenges head-on will almost certainly be a nightmare. You can spot a leader who has lost the mindset battle. They are exhausted, frazzled, bitter and erratic. Such a leader has surrendered to what they see as their fate. They hate everyone and everything. Before long, morale erodes, and those negative emotions start to take hold within their team.

There is a lot of material on the topic of mindset. Unfortunately, a large chunk of this information is challenging to navigate. I believe it is because mindset can be the hardest thing to see. You cannot touch it and, unlike behaviour, you cannot always see it in action. Your mindset is so deeply ingrained in who you are that you cannot reflect on it without bias. It is much more than your personality and preferences. Some would say it can be like trying to see the wood for the trees.

While the *Macquarie Dictionary* defines mindset as 'a particular mental framework of attitudes, expectations and prejudices', I have come to think of mindset as the attitudes, beliefs and expectations that underpin how you engage with the world. Positive or negative, your mindset will impact the way you engage with others and face challenges and opportunities. Working with leaders for many years, I have seen firsthand that a negative mindset can be like rust – the only element potent enough to destroy iron. Your mindset will fuel your leadership energy. It is the sole determinant of how you react to information and your environment. Mindset is crucial because you are likely completely unaware of it.

Your lack of technical strengths will not necessarily derail your effectiveness. A negative mindset, however, most certainly will.

Dr Carol Dweck, an American psychologist and the author of *Mindset: How You Can Fulfill Your Potential*, invested decades of research into the power of mindset. Her TED Talk, 'The power of believing you can improve', has been viewed more than 12 million times. In her bestselling book, Dweck explains that there are two mindsets – a fixed mindset and a growth mindset. A fixed mindset, according to Dweck, comes from the belief that your qualities are set in stone. You are who you are. You believe your intelligence, creativity, talents and personality are fixed and cannot be developed. On the other hand, a growth mindset comes from the belief that your qualities can be cultivated and nurtured through effort. Those with a growth mindset believe that their talents, interests, temperament and aptitude can change and grow through application and experience.

Dweck suggests that those who possess a fixed mindset are more inclined to favour familiar tasks to perform very well, establishing a reputation for accuracy and reliability. An individual with a fixed mindset will shy away from a challenge and be less resilient in the face of failure. Individuals with a growth mindset embrace learning and see challenges as an avenue for improvement. A leader with a growth mindset drives innovation.

OLD DOG, NEW TRICKS?

Imagine two leaders. Let's name them Bob and Jude. We will assume they both work in the same organisation. Bob and Jude are charged with the leadership of teams of similar size and expertise across portfolios that are equally complex.

Bob is sometimes known as the 'no!' man. He sees challenges and the potential for failure as something to actively avoid. Bob never puts his hand up to take on new tasks or be involved in new projects. Bob sees that time invested in expanding his skills and experience would provide very little to no tangible benefit to his career. Bob considers any effort to be fruitless. He limits peer-level engagement to avoid the threat of disagreement. Bob actively discourages innovation, highlighting mistakes to prevent a recurrence. It is hard to keep up with the movements within his team. Some call his department the revolving door of the organisation. There always seems to be a new face.

Jude, on the other hand, is a vibrant leader. Full of vision and possibility, Jude loves a good challenge. Even just a minute with Jude in the tearoom, if you are ever stuck, solves the problem. She loves to grow, learn and share. Jude is always volunteering to join new projects and committees and diving headfirst into activities that will stretch her skills. It's remarkable how she gets everything done. Jude only recently returned to her portfolio after a 12-month stint leading a team outside her technical expertise. Not only did she enjoy learning about a new and exciting part of the business, but she was able to mentor one of her team members while they acted in her substantive role. Jude actively shares her insights of failure and setbacks to encourage her team and peers to try new things. 'Innovation does not happen when we remain comfortable' is her mantra. Jude is an active member of the leadership team, engaging in authentic discussion. Jude has grown as a leader, learning from the insights and viewpoints of others. Because of this, Jude believes in investing in her team to ensure they have everything they need to be the best they can be.

Both leaders operate under the same organisational values and culture, yet their views of the world could not be more different. Who would you rather work for? Which leader are you?

MINDSET ISN'T RESILIENCE

No! Mindset is not *just* resilience. I defined mindset as the attitudes, beliefs and expectations that underpin how we engage with the world. I define resilience as our ability to recover quickly from a setback. Resilience is much like grit. It is your level of persistence. The plethora of research on the topic defines resilience as the process of adapting well in the face of adversity, challenge or significant stress. Some say it is how well you bounce back from a difficult circumstance. Mindset, therefore, determines your capacity for resilience. Your mindset provides the foundation that you leverage in the face of adversity. How you view the world and what is happening to you will significantly influence how you respond.

Leaders who attempt to build resilience in their people after a setback or failure are much like skydiving instructors teaching beginner skydivers how to safely land after their first jump. Focus instead on building your team's growth mindset. Resilience is an excellent skill to have yet is commonly misdiagnosed as the solution to a destructive, fixed mindset. Unless you change your view of the world, you cannot simply keep getting up again. It is unsustainable and can lead to burnout.

CHANGE YOUR MIND, CHANGE YOUR DIRECTION

You may know the fable of the tortoise and the hare. I believe the main principles derived from the parable are instructive for aspiring impactful leaders.

'I am faster than any animal in the woods,' the hare boasted, surrounded by his animal friends. 'No-one is as quick as I am.' Overhearing the hare, the tortoise suggested that he knew of someone who could beat him in a race. 'Who?' questioned the hare. The tortoise replied confidently, 'Me.'

As the hare recovered from fits of laughter, he accepted the tortoise's challenge. 'Let's do it. I will race you, and I will win!' The animals of the woods gathered and marked the course. The tortoise plodded to the starting line, the hare bounding over to join him. On their marks, the hare told himself that he was sure to win. The tortoise said to himself that as long as he participated, he had a chance to win. As soon as the words 'Ready, set, go!' were screamed, the hare was off, leaving a cloud of dust to envelop the tortoise who slowly, one step after the other, made his way. The hare could no longer be seen in the distance.

It was a hot day and, looking back, the hare couldn't even spot the tortoise. The shade of a nearby tree was too attractive. 'I'll just have a quick nap. The tortoise will never catch up.' Woken by the growing roar of a cheering crowd, the hare saw the tortoise ahead, approaching the finish line. 'What? But how?' the hare asked in panic. Despite his ability to hop at great speed, the hare could not catch the tortoise. The animals of the woods celebrated and cheered the tortoise, astonished by his victory. The hare, embarrassed, quietly retreated.

The hare believed in his innate ability. His mindset was fixed. The tortoise thought that he needed to persist and work hard if he was going to win. The tortoise did not fear losing, even knowing that the odds were stacked heavily against him. The tortoise had a growth mindset.

The most popular real-world, although admittedly not contemporary, example of the tortoise and the hare is the business success of the Wright brothers. It was the late 1890s and Samuel Pierpont Langley, an American physicist, inventor and aviation pioneer, was working with government support and enormous public exposure to create powered controllable flight. Langley had all the potential to make the dream a reality. He boasted publicly about what he could do. What's more, he had the financial backing to almost guarantee his success. Langley is the hare. He held two grand public attempts to showcase his invention on 7 October and 8 December 1903. Launched from a catapult, both creations fell from the sky. The Wright brothers, Wilbur and Orville, were bicycle shop owners. They are the tortoise in this story. Investors were not interested in the brothers' outrageous dreams. Despite the absence of external interest, they soldiered on. Their growth mindset and perseverance led to the ultimate discovery of man-machined flight. Just nine days after Langley's second failed attempt, the Wright brothers flew their biplane to almost no fanfare. They found success because they focused on the obstacles to flight.

Dweck's body of work provides excellent insight into both fixed and growth mindsets. Her research helped divide the population into glass-half-full and glass-half-empty thinkers. But your mindset is more than just fixed or growth. It was once believed the brain did not change beyond puberty – that it deteriorated as we aged. Research over the last 30 years has debunked this theory, demonstrating the untapped power of the brain. Dr Celeste Campbell, a respected American neuropsychologist, says, 'From the time the brain begins to develop in utero until the day we die, the connections among the cells in our brains reorganize in response to our changing needs. This dynamic process allows us to learn from and adapt to different experiences.'

A leader with a growth mindset sees opportunity, even during times of crisis. They will not be found in the foetal position under their desk, convinced all effort has been wasted. They do not seek to assign blame. They are focused on accelerating the growth of their team to overcome any challenge that they might face in the future.

As we experience new things or think differently, the brain develops new neurological pathways. When we continue to experience and think differently, these new neurological pathways soon become hardwired. These new connections become easier to use and facilitate the shift from a fixed to a growth mindset. It all sounds very simple, right?

THE POWER OF 'YET'

You would have been able to identify people you know in my example of Bob and Jude earlier. With reflection, you may be able to see yourself. Are you Bob, or are you Jude? If you are Bob, it can feel almost impossible to see the possibilities. Positive self-talk is not enough to leverage a growth mindset. But one word is mighty – 'yet'. By 'yet', I mean that the desired outcome has not happened, but with some effort, there is still a great chance that it will. The word 'yet' provides a bridge between our current reality and the desired state. This bridge helps to change our view of the world around us. It helps us change our beliefs, attitudes and expectations. The power of 'yet' allows us to reach our full potential.

Pondering the 'yet' allows you to reframe the situation. Rather than declare the end of the world, reframe to expand possibilities. Ask yourself, 'what is the yet?'

The environment in which we operate can nurture or hinder our mindset. I have worked with organisations that have pinned posters about growth mindset in tearooms, yet continually stifle innovation and draw attention to mistakes. Learning is not considered a part of the employee growth journey. Is your environment conducive to a growth mindset? Do you lead a team where discovery, success, failure and learning are encouraged and shared, or do you insist the team sticks with core roles and expertise?

Is reliable better than radical?

Fourteen ways to build a growth mindset

Here are a few tips I have provided to clients to help them build a growth mindset. Yes, some may seem a little wacky. They are, however, focused on experiencing something new. Leadership is about being comfortable to be uncomfortable. The process of building new neurological pathways, and allowing the old ones to become overgrown, takes time.

1. **Flip it.** What is the hidden opportunity that you might not be able to see from your current perspective?

2. **Try a new cuisine.** Immerse yourself in the cultural experience. Find the cultural hotspot near you for that cuisine. Eat at the restaurant. Avoid takeaway or home delivery.

3. **Be curious**. Reframe the situation. Only ask questions. 'What if...?' 'How could...?'

4. **Leverage the power of 'yet'**. Where could you start? What might need to happen first?

5. **Be optimistic, even when the odds are against you.** Optimists are happier, healthier and wealthier.

6. **Travel.** It doesn't have to be far. Choose a town or city you have never been to before. Ditch the car and wander the streets. Discover. Explore. Experience.

7. **Dance**. Even if it is alone at home, with the music loud. Feel the music.

8. **Create**. Art is a great way to explore and express yourself. Paint, sculpt, sketch, photograph, write.

9. **Learn something.** It might be a new hobby or a new skill. Perhaps a musical instrument?

10. **Read a fiction novel.** Take your mind on an adventure from the comfort of your favourite armchair.

11. **Listen to your language.** Negative language shuts all doors to possibility. Replace words like 'fail' with 'learn', and 'hopeless' with 'exciting'.

12. **Celebrate your success with others.** Motivate yourself and others by inviting them to share in your success.

13. **Visit a museum, gallery or exhibition on your own.** Explore. Sit. Step back. When my wife and I travelled to Florence, Italy, we visited the statue of David. Most tourists made a beeline directly to the statue, pressing against the rail to get a good glimpse and the obligatory selfie. We chose to visit the galleries with a tour guide who told us to stand at the opposite end of the hall and observe the statue. From a distance, you see so much more than what you can up close. The statue takes on a different presence from afar. On your solo exploration, take a step back. How much more do you see?

14. **Assemble jigsaw puzzles.** Over time you will start to recognise patterns amongst the pieces to complete the picture faster.

CONCLUSION

In this chapter, we covered the concept of the power of mindset. The way you view the world is deeply ingrained. It is the product of your upbringing, values, beliefs and life experiences. This is by far the greatest challenge. You are courageous. You are gritty. Get uncomfortable. Be brilliant!

Final thoughts

Often it is not about becoming a new person, but becoming a person you were meant to be, and already are, but don't know how to be.

– Heath L Buckmaster

I wrote *Just Lead!* to inspire you – the next generation of leaders – to emerge. Leadership is an occupation and not simply an elevated level of management.

My hope is that *Just Lead!* will help you become a better leader. Become the leader you yearn to be – a leader who can change the world. By improving your leadership skills, you can develop into an impactful leader who is more influential, less stressed, more empowered and aspires to leave a legacy.

Leadership is a dance. In this book, we have explored the pillars of impactful leadership: awareness, clarity and energy. I asserted that you must first understand and lead yourself before you can lead others. United by a clear *why*, we navigated amplifying the contribution of others and shining a light on their aspirations. Impactful leaders use stories to bridge the gap over uncertain waters connecting certainty and ambiguity. You read about finding your courage to fuel your leadership energy. Now that you are aware of the three pillars of impactful leadership, if you can begin to incorporate these into your daily practice, you are well on the way to becoming the leader you aspire to be.

You could potentially be the biggest obstacle to your success as a leader. Don't be afraid to be deeply reflective at times. Recognising that your approach to leadership could benefit from reflection is the first step to increasing your influence.

Just Lead! is a call to unleash your brilliance. Leadership is a lifelong journey. Keep learning and growing, empowering and developing others. Decide what you want your legacy to be and go for it!

Acknowledgements

Thank you to God, who blesses me with the gift of sharing the journey of leadership with so many people.

Thank you to Kath Walters for helping me turn a mass of ideas in my head into a book I am proud of.

Thank you to my early readers, Dr Dennis Gilles, Sue Anderson, Jenny Dahlstrom and Penny Lyall, who provided invaluable feedback that shaped the final version of this book.

Thank you to the team at Publish Central, especially my editor Brooke Lyons, who made the adventure of self-publishing so easy.

Thank you to every leader in my career, both good and bad. You have made me the leader I am today and provided a wealth of material for this book.

And finally, to my wife, Mimi, whose support made *Just Lead!* a reality – thank you for believing in me.

About the author

When leadership is the deciding factor, it's critical to learn from an expert who has seen it all go right and all go wrong.

Dale Monk is the founder of the Ministry of Leadership, a leadership and business mentoring practice specialising in harnessing the untapped potential of leaders and teams.

With more than 15 years of experience in senior leadership roles, Dale has seen firsthand the impact of both good and bad leadership on organisations, team morale and individuals. Compassionately confrontational, he has a passion for assisting others to learn, grow and become influential, impactful leaders.

Dale is a dynamic thought leader and an expert in helping technical experts shine as brilliant leaders.

WORK WITH DALE

Dale wrote *Just Lead!* to share the proven tools and strategies he uses with his clients to enhance their leadership impact. If you're hungry for more, you're in luck!

We all have blind spots. Sometimes we need a fresh perspective and some honest guidance to keep us on track – a trusted mentor to help us through the most difficult of our leadership challenges.

Dale knows what it takes to lead a team with impact. His proven framework has helped countless leaders just like you increase their influence, reduce their effort and advance their career. Dale knows how to leverage the right skills to positively impact teams and organisations.

Dale strips back the learnt leadership behaviours that derail success, helping you leverage your unique motivational profile to be an authentic and impactful leader.

Dale's energy, humour and passion, along with his winning influence formula, is the perfect mix to help leaders and teams excel. His ability to synthesise and disrupt naturally results in innovation. If you and/or your organisation can't seem to make your agenda stick, get Dale involved!

To learn more about Dale and his programs, visit www.ministryofleadership.com or send an email to hello@ministryof-leadrship.com.

References

The impactful leader's manifesto

Hougaard, R 2018, 'The Real Crisis In Leadership', Forbes, forbes.com/sites/rasmushougaard/2018/09/09/the-real-crisis-in-leadership/?sh=42936c763ee4.

Zaleznik, A 1977, 'Managers and Leaders: Are They Different?', *Harvard Business Review*, hbr.org/2004/01/managers-and-leaders-are-they-different.

Westfall, C 2019, 'Leadership Development Is A $366 Billion Industry: Here's Why Most Programs Don't Work', Forbes, forbes.com/sites/chriswestfall/2019/06/20/leadership-development-why-most-programs-dont-work/?sh=6417100061de.

Kellerman, B 2004, *Bad Leadership: What It Is, How It Happens, Why It Matters*, Harvard Business Review Press.

Leimbach, M 2021, 'The times they are a changing...', *Training Magazine*, May, p. 26.

Recruiter.com 2011, 'The cost of a bad hire [infographic]', recruiter.com/i/the-cost-of-a-bad-hire-infographic.

Challenger, Gray & Christmas, Inc 2019, *2019 Year-End CEO Report*, challengergray.com/blog/2019-year-end-ceo-report-160-ceos-out-december-highest-annual-quarterly-totals.

The Ken Blanchard Companies 2020, *7 Ways Poor Leaders Are Costing Your Company Money*, resources.kenblanchard.com/ebooks/7-ways-poor-leaders-are-costing-your-company-money.

Huhman, H 2018, 'Research Shows That Your First-Time Managers Aren't Ready to Lead. Now, What?', Entrepreneur, entrepreneur.com/article/309052.

George, B, Sims, P, McLean, A & Mayer, D 2007, 'Discovering Your Authentic Leadership', *Harvard Business Review*, hbr.org/2007/02/discovering-your-authentic-leadership.

Chapter 1: First, lead yourself

Goleman, D 2005, *Emotional Intelligence: Why It Can Matter More Than IQ*, Bantam.

Flaum, JP 2018, *When it comes to business, leadership, nice guys finish first*, greenpeakpartners.com/wp-content/uploads/2018/09/Green-Peak_Cornell-University-Study_What-predicts-success.pdf.

Bradberry, T & Tasler, N 2020, 'Increasing Your Salary with Emotional Intelligence', TalentSmartEQ, talentsmarteq.com/articles/Increasing-Your-Salary-with-Emotional-Intelligence-983916766-p-1.html.

Eurich, T 2018, Insight: *The Surprising Truth About How Others See Us, How We See Ourselves, and Why the Answers Matter More Than We Think*, Currency.

Seo, M & Feldman Barrett, L 2007, 'Being Emotional During Decision Making—Good or Bad? An Empirical Investigation', *Academy of Management Journal*, 50(4): 923–940.

Chapter 2: Understanding others

Rozovsky, J 2015, 'The five keys to a successful Google team', re:Work, rework.withgoogle.com/blog/five-keys-to-a-successful-google-team.

Fortune 2021, '100 Best Companies to Work For', fortune.com/best-companies/2021.

Mann, CR 1918, *A Study of Engineering Education*, Carnegie Foundation.

Green M & McGill E 2011, *The State of the Industry Report*, American Society of Training and Development.

DeakinCo. 2017, *Soft skills for business success*, www2.deloitte.com/content/dam/Deloitte/au/Documents/Economics/deloitte-au-economics-deakin-soft-skills-business-success-170517.pdf.

Chapter 3: But, why?

Harvard Business Review 2015, *The Business Case for Purpose*, hbr.org/sponsored/2015/10/the-business-case-for-purpose.

Gallup 2021, State of the Global Workplace: 2021 Report, gallup.com/workplace/349484/state-of-the-global-workplace.aspx.

Sinek, S 2009, 'How great leaders inspire action', TED, ted.com/talks/simon_sinek_how_great_leaders_inspire_action?language=en.

Buettner, D 2010, *The Blue Zones: Lessons for Living Longer from the People Who've Lived the Longest*, National Geographic.

LinkedIn 2016, *Purpose at Work: 2016 Global Report*, business.linkedin.com/content/dam/me/business/en-us/talent-solutions/resources/pdfs/purpose-at-work-global-report.pdf.

Imperative 2020, 2019 Workforce Purpose Index, 2019wpi.com.

Bamboo HR 2018, '3 Key Benefits of Employee Engagement [Statistics Included]', bamboohr.com/blog/major-benefits-employee-engagement.

Baldoni, J 2013, 'Employee Engagement Does More than Boost Productivity', *Harvard Business Review*, hbr.org/2013/07/employee-engagement-does-more.

Harvard Business Review 2015, *The Business Case for Purpose*, hbr.org/sponsored/2015/10/the-business-case-for-purpose.

Craig, N & Snook, SA 2014, 'From Purpose to Impact', Harvard Business Review, hbr.org/2014/05/from-purpose-to-impact.

Gallup 2016, 'How Millennials Want to Work and Live', gallup.com/workplace/238073/millennials-work-live.aspx.

Chapter 5: Leading safely through ambiguity

Pijnacker, L 2019, 'HR analytics: role clarity impacts performance', Effectory, effectory.com/knowledge/hr-analytics-role-clarity-impacts-performance.

Korn Ferry 2015, 'Leading through ambiguity', focus.kornferry.com/leadership-and-talent/leading-through-ambiguity.

Robbins, M 2017, *The 5 Second Rule: The Fastest Way To Change Your Life*, Permuted Press.

Philip Tetlock, P & Gardner, D 2015, *Superforecasting: The Art and Science of Prediction*, Crown.

Chapter 6: The power of stories

Paul, AM 2012, 'Your Brain on Fiction', *The New York Times*, nytimes.com/2012/03/18/opinion/sunday/the-neuroscience-of-your-brain-on-fiction.html.

Owens, A 2021, 'Tell Me All I Need to Know About Oxytocin', Psycom, psycom.net/oxytocin.

Dolan, G 2017, *Stories for Work: The Essential Guide to Business Storytelling*, John Wiley & Sons Australia.

Covey, SR 2004, *The 7 Habits of Highly Effective People: Powerful Lessons in Personal Change*, Free Press.

Box Office Mojo n.d., boxofficemojo.com.

Connor, J 2013, 'The Pixar Pitch! Telling your Story Crisply and with Clarity in order to Compel Action', Working Differently, workingdifferently.org/working-differently-blog/the-pixar-pitch-telling-your-story-crisply-and-with-clarity-in-order-to-compel-action.

Coats, E 2012, '22 Story Rules', Twitter, https://twitter.com/lawnrocket.

Price, DA 2011, 'Pixar story rules (one version)', The Pixar Touch, pixartouchbook.com/blog/2011/5/15/pixar-story-rules-one-version.html.

Pink, DH 2013, *To Sell Is Human: The Surprising Truth About Moving Others*, Riverhead Books.

Chapter 7: Pioneering leadership

Distefano, M n.d., 'Alan Mulally: The Man Who Saved Ford', Korn Ferry, kornferry.com/insights/briefings-magazine/issue-20/alan-mulally-man-who-saved-ford.

George, B 2017, 'Courage: The Defining Characteristic Of Great Leaders', Forbes, forbes.com/sites/hbsworkingknowledge/2017/04/24/

courage-the-defining-characteristic-of-great-leaders/?sh=347fa59511ca.

Capgemini Consulting 2015, *When Digital Disruption Strikes: How Can Incumbents Respond?*, slideshare.net/capgemini/digital-disruption-44929928.

Chapter 8: Get gritty!

Duckworth, A 2016, *Grit: The Power of Passion and Perseverance*, Scribner Book Company.

Kannangara, CS et al. 2018, 'All That Glitters Is Not Grit: Three Studies of Grit in University Students', *Frontiers in Psychology*.

Middleton, A 2019, *The Fear Bubble: Harness Fear and Live without Limits*, HarperCollins.

Gladwell, M 2011, *Outliers: The Story of Success*, Back Bay Books.

Mischel, W et al. 1990, 'Preschool Delay of Gratification: Identifying Diagnostic Conditions', *Developmental Psychology*, vol. 26, no. 6, pp. 978–986.

Chapter 9: Lead at your best

Dweck, C 2013, *Mindset: How You Can Fulfill Your Potential*, Constable & Robinson.

Ackerman, CE 2021, 'What is Neuroplasticity? A Psychologist Explains', PositivePsychology, positivepsychology.com/neuroplasticity.

—

www.ingramcontent.com/pod-product-compliance
Lightning Source LLC
Chambersburg PA
CBHW071419210326
41597CB00020B/3568